Pattern-drafting for Fashion
the basics

Bloomsbury Visual Arts
An imprint of Bloomsbury Publishing Plc
Imprint previously known as A&C Black Visual Arts

50 Bedford Square   1385 Broadway
London   New York
WC1B 3DP   NY 10018
UK   USA

www.bloomsbury.com

**BLOOMSBURY and the Diana logo are trademarks
of Bloomsbury Publishing Plc**

First published in France in 2008 Éditions Eyrolles
61, bd Saint-Germain
75240 Paris Cedex 05
www.editions-eyrolles.com
Printed by Bloomsbury Visual Arts in 2011
Reprinted 2015

Original title:
Le Modélisme de mode
Volume 1: Coupes à plat, les bases
© 2008 Groupe Eyrolles, Paris, France

Copyright © 2011 Teresa Gilewska

British Library Cataloguing-in-Publication Data
A catalogue record for this book is available from the British Library.

ISBN: PB: 978-1-4081-2990-6

Coordination: Florence Daniel
Graphic design and page layout: Chantal Guézet
Design English-language edition: Penny Mills
With thanks to Andrea Gould

Printed and bound in China

Teresa Gilewska

Pattern-drafting for Fashion: the basics

Bloomsbury Visual Arts
An imprint of Bloomsbury Publishing Plc

B L O O M S B U R Y
LONDON · NEW DELHI · NEW YORK · SYDNEY

Contents

Foreword

This book is the result of 30 years of reflection and exploration in to the art of dressmaking. Whether teaching my numerous students in Poland, France or China, or even beginners who just delight in making their own wardrobe, I have wanted to help people realise that the creation of a garment is not just down to chance but to design! Like the body, the garment must follow precise rules of architecture, to which even the most experienced couturiers must adhere.

Far from being a hindrance, these rules of construction are easy to apply if one is given step-by-step instructions. Too often, I have seen dress-makers using block templates (pattern blocks from UK size 10 or 12 that serve as the basis of their work) without fully understanding the structural evolution of the garment they are making. Without wishing to reject these methods, I believe that it is infinitely more desirable to have the block in one's mind.

This is why in *Pattern-drafting for Fashion* you will not find a pattern that is ready to 'copy and cut-out', but you will find all the necessary instructions enabling you to make garments, while at the same time understanding the detailed construction of a skirt, blouse, jacket etc. You will then be able to make all your basics both simply and logically.

Do not be tempted by short-cuts; it is only by fully understanding that progression is made, which in turn means you will be able to make your garments better! In order to appeal to your creativity I have also included chapters detailing necklines, collars, sleeves, pockets and so on. Once you have made your basic block you will be able to modify and personalise your design.

I wanted this book to be more than just a method, rather an apprenticeship tool of how to logically understand and decipher the structure of a garment.

Teresa Gilewska

General Points

This first volume in the *Pattern-drafting for Fashion* series demonstrates how to construct a flat pattern by teaching the simple, necessary elements required.

The pattern-drafting technique is thorough and detailed. The designs are accompanied by descriptive diagrams that show how to make a garment and, most importantly, how to understand its construction.

The method developed in this book is accessible to everyone, whether they are a professional or amateur dressmaker.

But before we enter into the subject in greater depth – pattern construction and the step-by-step descriptions of each design – we are going to consider some general points: body measurements, standard size charts and two-dimensional patterns.

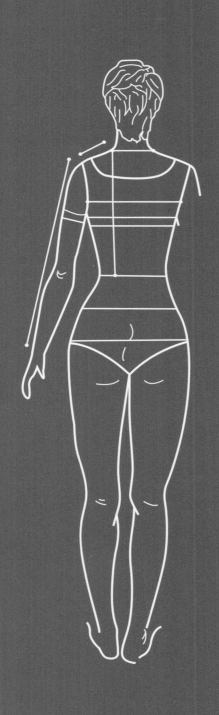
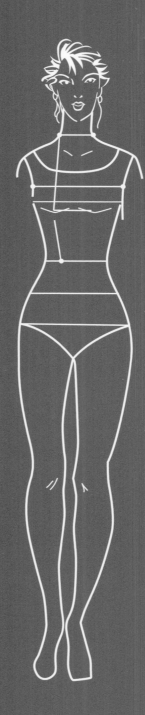

Body measurements

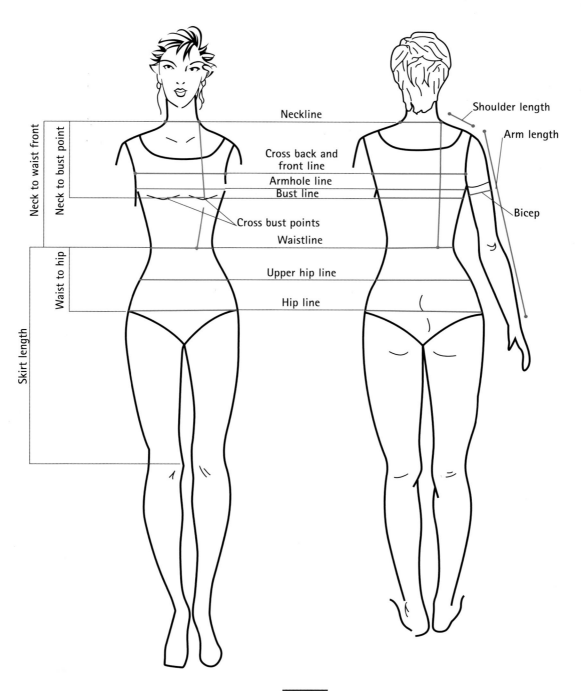

Labels on figure:

- Neckline
- Shoulder length
- Arm length
- Cross back and front line
- Armhole line
- Bust line
- Bicep
- Cross bust points
- Waistline
- Upper hip line
- Hip line
- Neck to waist front
- Neck to bust point
- Waist to hip
- Skirt length

FIG. 1

Whatever the design or size, it is advisable to make a basic pattern first and then add any alterations. It is important to take the measurements correctly before starting. First of all, find the position of the waistline by lightly tying a tape around the hollow area just above the hip bone. This line will serve as the guide for the length measurements.

Do not add any ease to these measurements as this will be applied to the basic pattern during its construction.

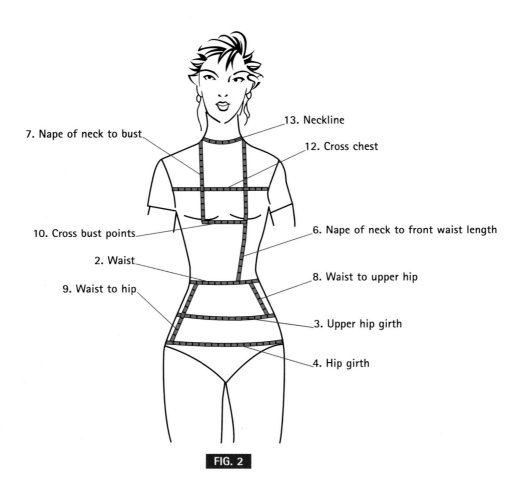

FIG. 2

1. Bust – place the tape around the widest part of the bust (see fig.4).

2. Waist – use the tape to find the slimmest part of the body (see fig.4).

3. Upper hip girth – about 10cm (4in.) below the waist.

4. Hip girth – about 20cm (8in.) below the waist at the widest part.

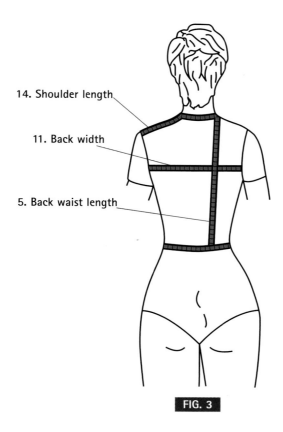

14. Shoulder length

11. Back width

5. Back waist length

FIG. 3

5. Back waist length – from the top of the shoulder at the nape, to the waist.

6. Front waist length – from the neck to the waist, passing over the most prominent part of the chest.

7. Neck to bust point – from the shoulder (at the neckline), to the bust point.

8. Waist to upper hip – 10cm (4in.) below the waist.

9. Waist to hip – 20cm (8in.) below the waist.

10. Cross bust points – from one bust point to the other.

11. Back width – from one sleeve pitch point to another.

12. Chest width – from one sleeve pitch point to another.

13. Neckline – at the base of the neck.

14. Shoulder length – from the neck to the position of the armhole.

15. Arm length – on a bent arm, from the shoulder to the elbow, then from the elbow to the wrist.

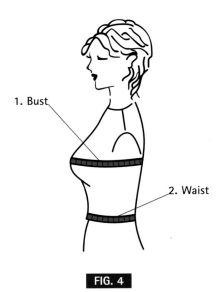

1. Bust

2. Waist

FIG. 4

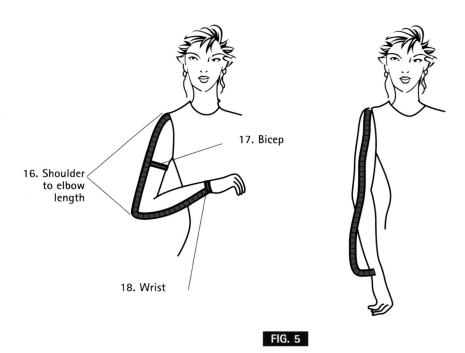

16. Shoulder to elbow length

17. Bicep

18. Wrist

FIG. 5

16. Length from top of arm to elbow.

17. Bicep – widest part of the upper arm.

18. Wrist

Standard size chart

Originally size charts (also called measurement tables) were composed of the average body measurements taken from 1,000 to 10,000 women by the IFTH (French Textile and Clothing Institute).

It is from these standard sizes that basic patterns are established.

However, this chart is not definitive, as in order to respond to customer needs, certain prêt-a-porter manufacturers specialising in a particular type of clothing have created their own charts with intermediary sizes or internal measurements.

Size charts can also vary for certain measurements that are disputed by the professionals. For example, the back waist length measurement is taken from either the middle of the nape of the neck or from the shoulder; this will naturally give two completely different readings due to the hollow between the shoulder blades.

There is therefore not one definitive size chart; on the contrary, each chart is adapted to a specific usage in conjunction with the basic pattern's construction methods.

The new survey for body measurements conducted in 2003–2004 revealed important modifications compared to that carried out previously in the 1950s.

The chart relates to a height of 168–172cm (66–68in.), and all measurements are given in centimetres.

UK SIZES	6	8	10	12	14	16	18	20	
USA SIZES	4	6	8	10	12	14	16	18	
AUSTRALIA SIZES	8	10	12	14	16	18	20	22	
EUROPE SIZES	34	36	38	40	42	44	46	48	Increment
1. Bust	80	84	88	92	96	100	104	106	4
2. Waist	58	62	66	70	74	78	82	86	4
3. Upper hip	73	77	81	85	89	93	97	101	4
4. Hip	84	88	92	96	100	104	108	112	4
5. Back waist length	41.25	41.5	41.75	42	42.25	42.5	42.75	43	0.25
6. Front waist length	44.2	44.8	45.4	46	46.6	47.2	47.8	48.4	0.6
7. Neck to bust point	25.5	26	26.5	27	27.5	28	28.5	29	0.5
8. Waist to upper hip	8.8	9	9.2	9.4	9.6	9.8	10	10.2	0.2
9. Waist to hip	19.25	19.5	19.75	20	20.25	20.5	20.75	21	0.25
10. Across bust points	18.5	19	19.5	20	20.5	21	21.5	22	0.5
11. Cross back width	34.5	35	35.5	36	36.5	37	37.5	38	0.5
12. Cross front width	33	33.5	34	34.5	35	35.5	36	36.5	0.5
13. Neckline	35	36	37	38	39	40	41	42	1
14. Shoulder length	13.4	13.6	13.8	14	14.2	14.4	14.6	14.8	0.2
15. Arm length	59	59	59	60	60	60	60	60	-
16. Shoulder to elbow length	35	35	35	35	35	35	35	35	-
17. Bicep	26	27	28	29	30	31	32	33	1
18. Wrist	15.25	15.75	16	16.25	16.5	16.5	16.75	17	0.25

Two-dimensional pattern

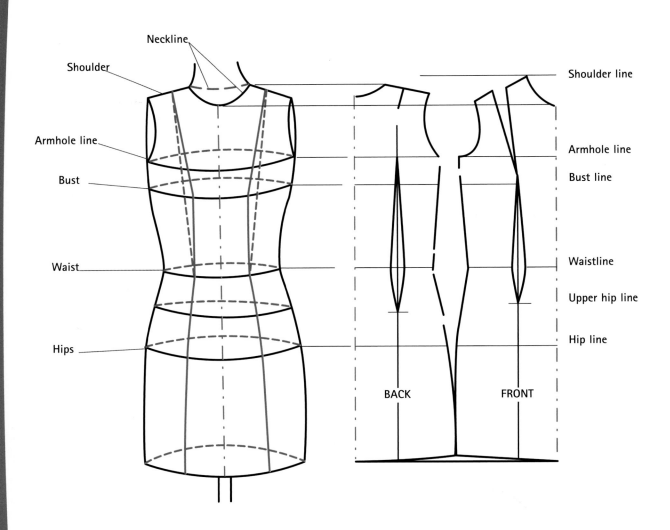

Neckline

Shoulder

Armhole line

Bust

Waist

Hips

Shoulder line

Armhole line

Bust line

Waistline

Upper hip line

Hip line

BACK

FRONT

Basic block construction.

FIG. 6

The pattern draft

The basic pattern is the two-dimensional development of the body shape and its proportions, as well as the positioning of darts, in reference to the given measurements.

> The correct fit of the garment on the body (without excess folds or restricted movement) depends on how well the basic pattern has been drafted.

Styling a garment for fashion does not pose too many problems when pattern making – the real challenge lies in achieving a good fit. The technique of pattern construction is not easily mastered. In order to acquire real skills, it is necessary to fully understand what you are doing and the development process.

There are three types of pattern construction:

1. prêt-à-porter – a pattern is based on standard measurements.
2. custom-made – a pattern that is based on measurements for an individual wearer.
3. haute couture – a pattern made by draping a toile onto a model of the client's body. (The model is normally made by taking a plaster cast of the body, which is then reconstructed in plastic.)

Some important points
The human body is permanently moving. In order to make a basic pattern for a comfortable garment, it is therefore very important to locate fixed points and stable lines in areas where there is movement.

Generally, the front length is longer than the back (because of the bust). For smaller sizes, this difference is on average 2–3cm (3–1¼in.), but for size 44, it is 4cm (1½in.) more. The construction of the bodice pattern must always begin with the centre back line (vertical line) and the waistline (horizontal line). If you begin the construction by marking the horizontal lines based on the front length this will result in a very long back without any possibility of reducing it with darts.

> **Don't forget!**
> Do not confuse the armhole line with the bust line! Generally, the bust line is positioned underneath the armhole. This difference is more noticeable on larger sizes or those with larger busts.

15

The bodice

There are many methods for making a bodice pattern, but the techniques shown here are particularly aimed at beginners.

It is very important to understand the basic structure of the bodice and to follow the processes set out here correctly, as this will help to ensure success.

In this book, the basic block is made without any tolerance or ease, that is, the extra allowance introduced for comfort. The tolerance will depend on the style, and will be added onto the finished basic pattern before the modifications.

Nor does it include seams. Since the basic block is a working tool that will be developed into the desired style, the seams will be added to the finished pattern.

Finally, the construction is made on one half of the back (half back) and one half of the front (half front). This is done to simplify the drafting and to ensure that a complete pattern is identical on both sides, the other two halves being obtained by simple symmetry.

Making the basic block

Whichever style has been chosen, the first step is to draft the basic bodice block using the measurements of the person for whom the garment is to be made.

Let us take the following example.

Back length = 44cm; front length = 46cm; bust circumference = 92cm.

The back and front patterns are made separately.

Start by drafting the half back pattern, then the half front pattern.

1. The back frame

First of all construct a frame: mark the centre line (the left vertical line in fig. 7 – the length for this example is 44cm), then the horizontal lines for the waistline (at the bottom) and the shoulder line (at the top).

The half width of the back is equal to the bust measurement divided by 4 and minus 1cm (⅜in.). In this example: (92cm ÷ 4) – 1cm = 22cm.

Then close up the back frame with a side line (vertical line on the right).

2. The front frame

Construct the front frame following the same principle (see fig. 7) but extending the waistline, then mark the centre front (vertical line on the right), the length for this example being 46cm.

The half width of the front is equal to the bust measurement divided by 4 plus 1cm (⅜in.). In this example: (92cm ÷ 4) + 1cm = 24cm.

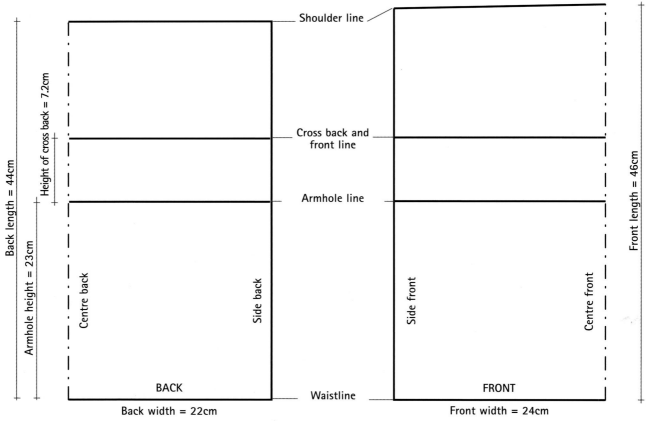

FIG. 7

3. The back neckline

For a perfectly fitting neckline, divide the neck girth by 16 to obtain its depth. For the width, divide the neck girth by 6.

For example: neck girth = 38cm

Neckline depth = 38cm ÷ 16 = 2.38cm

Neckline width = 38cm ÷ 6 = 6.3cm

Measure 1.5cm (⅝in.) at the right angle made by the depth and width of the neckline.

Then, using a French curve or Patternmaster, mark the curve of the neckline (see fig. 8).

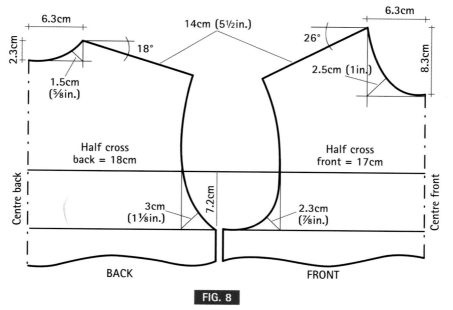

FIG. 8

4. The front neckline

Width of front neckline = width of back neckline

To obtain the depth of the front neckline, divide the neck girth by 6 then add 2cm (¾in.).

For example: neckline girth = 38cm (15in.)

Neckline depth = (38cm ÷ 6) + 2 = 8.3cm.

Measure 2.5cm (1in.) at the right angle where the depth and the width of the neckline bisect.

Then, using a French curve, mark the curve of the neckline (fig. 8).

5. The shoulder

On the shoulder line, use a protractor to measure an 18° angle for the back and 26° angle for the front. Then extend the shoulder length along these lines. (For example, in fig. 8 the shoulder length = 14cm.)

6. The armhole

To determine the height of the armhole, divide the back length by 2 then add 1cm (⅜in.) For example, in fig. 7 armhole height = (44cm ÷ 2) + 1 = 23cm.

Mark the armhole line 23cm above the waistline for the back and the front frame.

7. Cross back line

There is one final reference point required in order to draft the complete armhole curve: the cross back height.

Cross back height = ([back length – armhole height – back neckline depth] ÷ 3) +1cm (⅜in.). In this example: ([44 – 23 – 2.38cm] ÷ 3) + 1cm = 7.2cm. Place the cross back line 7.2cm above the armhole line (fig. 8).

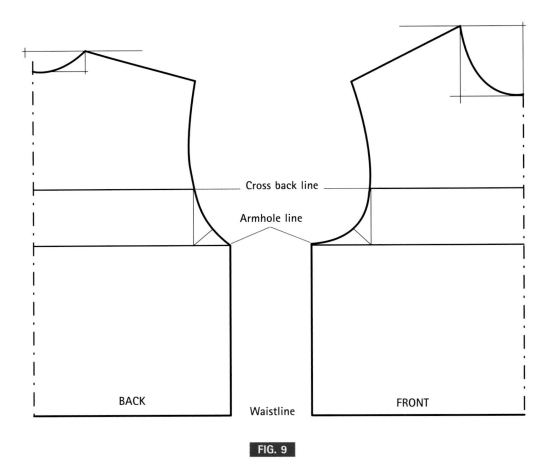

Cross back line

Armhole line

BACK

Waistline

FRONT

FIG. 9

At the right angle where the armhole and cross back height lines intersect, mark 3cm (1⅛in.) for the back and 2.3cm (⅞in.) for the front. Finish the pattern by using a French curve to trace the armholes (figs 8 and 9).

When constructing a folded pattern (half back and half front) remember the measurements in fig. 8 are half cross back.
For example: cross back = 36cm; half cross back = 36 ÷ 2 = 18cm; cross front = 34cm; half cross front = 34 ÷ 2 = 17cm.

Making darts on the basic block

It may be necessary to add different darts to the basic pattern.

1. The basic dart or 'strap' dart
To make this dart, some important measurements must be calculated and marked onto the half front pattern: the chest height and half cross bust.

For example chest height = 27cm, half cross bust = 19cm ÷ 2 = 9.5cm.

Next mark the first dart line starting from the centre of the shoulder line down to the bust point. Calculate the dart measurement described below and mark the second dart line that distance from the first:

Dart measurement = 1/20th of the chest girth

For example: if chest girth is 92cm, then dart measurement is 92cm ÷ 20 = 4.6cm.

The second dart line must be identical in length to the first. To adjust the shoulder line (after closing the dart) mark the second part of the shoulder line at an angle of 72° from the second dart line.

Add the dart suppression amount (the quantity of fabric needed to be absorbed by the dart) to the armhole (see fig. 10), and mark the armhole curve as previously described.

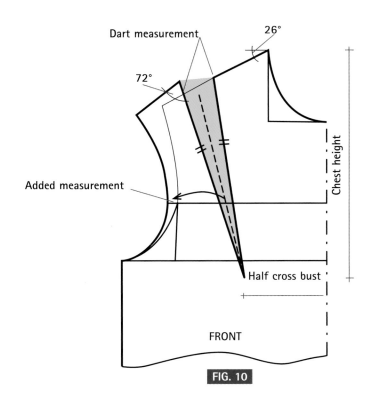

FIG. 10

2. Waist darts

The difference between the chest and waist measurements determines the dart's suppression (quantity of fabric needed to be absorbed by the dart). This measurement must be divided between seven basic darts (see fig. 11):
– Two front darts, placed on the vertical line determined by the cross bust measurement. These are not normally more than 3cm (1⅛in.).
– Two back darts (the dart's axis is a quarter of the back's width). This measurement is normally no bigger than 3cm (1⅛in.).
– Two side darts. Half measurement is normally no bigger than 4cm (1⅝in.).
– One centre back dart. The half measurement is generally 1–2cm (⅜–¾in.).

Do not make the darts too big or the garment will become distorted.

Example of how to calculate the balance of darts for a chest girth of 92cm and a waist girth of 68cm:
– Chest girth minus waist girth is 92cm – 68cm = 24cm
– 24cm ÷ 2 = 12cm (so 12cm will be the dart intake for a half pattern)
– 12cm –1cm (half measurement of centre back dart) = 11cm
– 11cm ÷ 4 = 2.75cm for each dart on average. This can be distributed as 2.5cm (1in.) for the back and front darts and 3cm (1⅛in.) (half measurement either side) for the side darts.
For example 1cm (half the measurement of the centre back dart) + 2.5cm (back dart) + 2.5cm (front dart) + 2 x 3cm (half of the measurement of the side darts) = 12cm (the amount of the dart suppression from the start).
Generally, the height of the back darts must not be higher than the cross back line. The height of the front darts can go up to the curve of the bust, allowing for 2cm (¾in.) rounded off over the bust point.

The distribution of the dart amounts will depend on the shape of the individual for whom the garment is made. If there is a large difference between the chest and waist girths then it is possible to suppress this by making several darts.

3. Back shoulder dart

The back shoulder dart is placed in the centre of the shoulder line at an angle of 90° to that line. (See fig. 11.)
Dart measurement = + or – 1cm (⅜in.); dart length = + or – 7cm (2¾in.).

It must be noted that this dart is rarely used in smaller sizes but will be needed for larger sizes to accommodate the curve at the top of the bust. When using heavy fabrics, for garments such as coats and jackets, using this type of dart allows for a quantity of material to be suppressed despite the inflexibility of the fabric. With lighter, more flexible fabrics there is no need to use this type of dart.

22

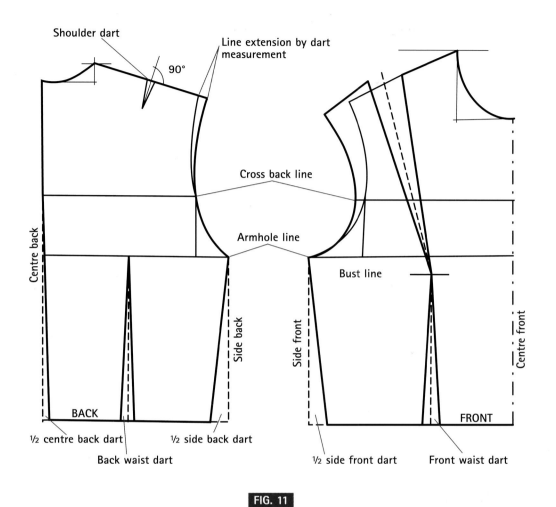

Shoulder dart

Line extension by dart measurement

90°

Cross back line

Armhole line

Centre back

Bust line

Side back

Side front

Centre front

BACK

FRONT

½ centre back dart

½ side back dart

Back waist dart

½ side front dart

Front waist dart

FIG. 11

The construction of the basic pattern has now been successfully completed.

This technique can be used to create a simple, precise working block from which, after alterations and fittings, successful patterns can be made.

Dart manipulation

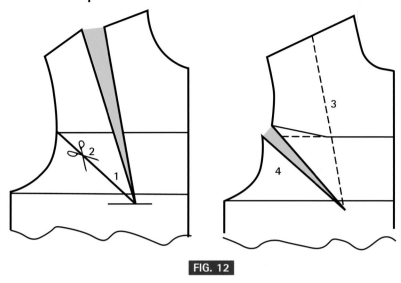

FIG. 12

In general, if a dart is needed on the front of a bodice, the usual procedure is to start with a basic dart to the shoulder seam. The dart can then be closed, and slashed open in the new position. This technique is quick and easy and allows an exact template of the dart to be produced.

1. Draw the dart line in its new position.
2. Slash it open as shown in fig. 12.
3. Close the shoulder dart, eliminating the cut out section.
4. Trace off the new dart.

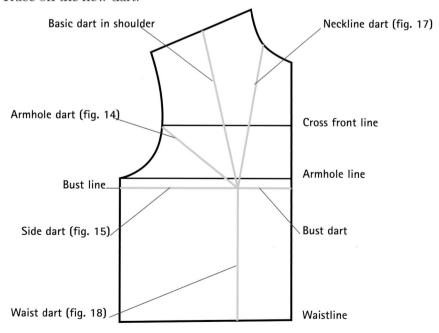

Positioning of bodice darts.

FIG. 13

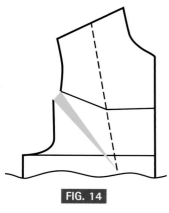

FIG. 14

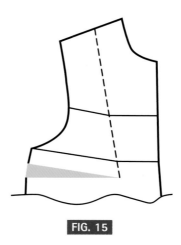

FIG. 15

Armhole dart
Normally this dart should not be drawn below the cross front line as the armhole curve is cut on the bias and has a tendency to slacken, which could distort the initial line.

Side dart
This dart is often used, positioned about 4cm (1⅝in.) underneath the armhole line.

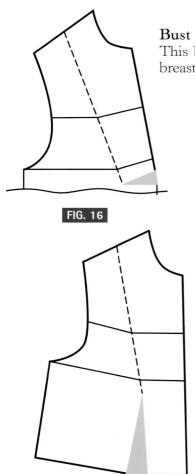

FIG. 16

Bust dart
This bust dart is positioned between the breasts (called a Dior dart).

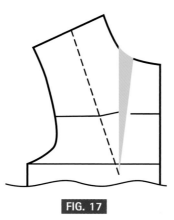

FIG. 17

Neckline dart
This dart can be hidden by the collar lapel or distributed evenly by gathers around the neckline. The dart is positioned in the centre of the neckline on the bias. This enlarges the neckline line so that it can be gathered as an attractive feature.

FIG. 18

Waist dart
This dart is used to define the waist. If there is a large amount of fabric to be suppressed then several darts will be necessary. Multiple darts can be a style feature. Note that a dart placed on the shallow curve of the neckline (too near to the centre front) can distort its shape.

25

Basic knitwear bodice

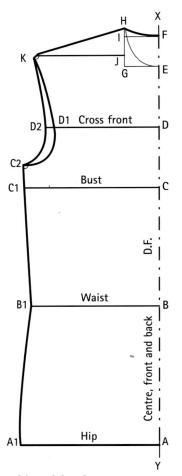

Mark the back and the front starting from the same vertical line, XY (centre back and front).

Place points A, B, C, D, E, and F so that AB = hip height, BE = front length, BF = back length, CE =½ BE (bust line), DE =½ CE (cross front and back line).

Mark perpendicular lines on XY from points A, B, C, D, E, F so AA1 = ¼ hip girth, BB1 = ¼ waist girth, CC1 = ¼ bust girth, DD1 =½ cross front, DD2 =½ cross back.

Front neckline curve

Draw EG and GH (⅙ of the neckline girth). At the middle of the right angle formed by EG/GH, measure 2.5cm (1in.). Then, using a French curve, trace the neckline curve HE, squaring off for 1.5cm (⅝in.) at the centre front.

Back neckline curve

Mark HI = 2.4cm (1in.). At the right angle formed by FI/IH, measure 2.3cm (⅞in.) and use a French curve to trace the back neckline curve HF, squaring off for 3cm (1⅛in.) from the centre back.

Shoulder line

GJ = 1/3 of GH. Mark the horizontal line JK, with HK being the shoulder length.

Side line

Using a French curve or Patternmaster, trace the curve A1B1. B1C2 = (front length + back length) ÷ 4 + 2.5cm (1in.). Join B1C2 passing by C1.

Front armhole

Using a French curve, join C2, D1, K, squaring off for 1.5cm (⅝in.) from C2.

Back armhole

Using a French curve, join C2, D2, K, squaring off for 1cm (⅜in.) from C2.

Trace off the front and back separately, using the mirror image of each pattern in order to obtain the other half.

This block can be used to construct all garments made in knitted fabric.

Tolerance

This is when the measurements you have taken from the wearer are increased to give more room to the garment. This will vary depending on the style, the amount of room desired or the amount of comfort required.

The first step to achieve a successful pattern must be to draft the basic block from the wearer's measurements, and then add the tolerance. This is because construction calculations that include tolerance are not always exact. (For example, the height of the cross back, the dart measurements or the neckline.)

The measurements given here correspond to the basic tolerance for a classic garment. They are therefore minimal.

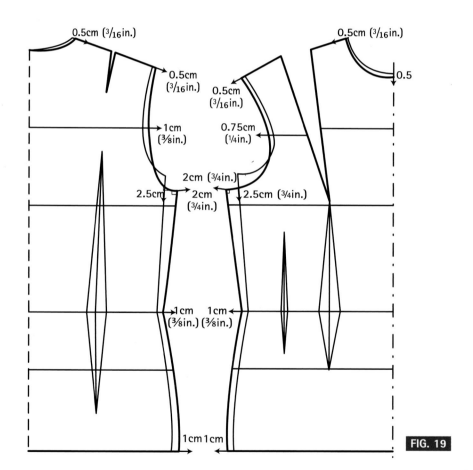

FIG. 19

Shoulder tolerance

The shoulder line must be raised and lengthened for garments with shoulder pads. For example, with a shoulder pad of 1cm (⅜in.) thickness, raise and lengthen the shoulder line by 1cm (⅜in.).

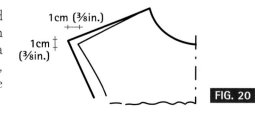

FIG. 20

Notches

These are small cut-outs, or nicks, about 3mm in length, which are placed at the edge of the fabric. There are two types of notches used in pattern making:

Balance notches indicate the position of a piece of fabric during assembly; they identify the back or the front of a sleeve, for example (see fig. 21). If a sleeve has no elbow shaping, balance notches are vital.

Sewing notches serve to line up two pieces of fabric during assembling by keeping them in the right position in relation to the horizontal and vertical lines. This helps to match the balance points of the garment. For example, with a princess-line dress, the notches must be positioned on the waist and bust lines of the two front pieces (see fig. 22).

The notches must be placed on the finished pattern, after the seam allowance has been added, and preserved throughout the cutting process so that they can be used to assemble the garment.

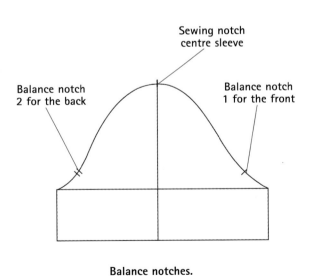

Sewing notch centre sleeve

Balance notch 2 for the back

Balance notch 1 for the front

Balance notches.

FIG. 21

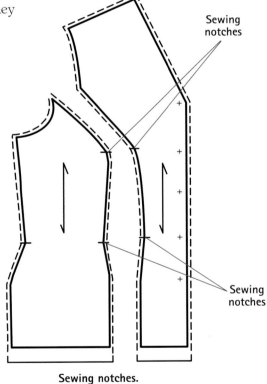

Sewing notches

Sewing notches

Sewing notches.

FIG. 22

Don't forget! Assembling a garment by eye, without any notches or location points, will result in a distorted garment.

Straightening out

In some styles, seams cut on the bias will need to be straightened so that the garment fits the body more smoothly. In a pattern cut on the straight grain, the cuves in the pattern are drawn for a perfect fit around the body. But when a pattern is cut on the bias, the natural stretch of the fabric is all that is needed to fit the the body; any curves on the pattern will be enlarged and stick out like 'ears'.

For example, with a princess-line dress, the point created where the waist and the sleeve darts meet is removed for a better fit on the bust line.

Generally, this small flat area depends on the size of the bust in question, and is achieved by shortening the dart lengths by approximately 2cm (¾in.) around the bust point (fig. 24).

Sleeve ease

This is an extra measurement added to the top part of the sleeve (fig. 23). It depends on the sleeve design and style of garment, and is more commonly used for visual effect than for comfort.

The armhole of the bodice serves as a support for the sleeve. Generally, the seam is 'flattened' towards the sleeve. When the garment is tried on the body, you will see that the natural roundness of the arm means that the top of the sleeve needs a bit of extra length adding to the measurement obtained using the girth and the depth of the armhole.

Examples of amounts of ease added to sleeves for different garments are as follows: straight shirt, 0.5–1cm (³⁄₁₆–⅜in.); blouse with darts, 1–2cm (⅜–¾in.); jacket with shoulder pads, 2–4cm (¾–1⅝in.).

Note that in this book the construction of the basic sleeve does not incorporate added ease.

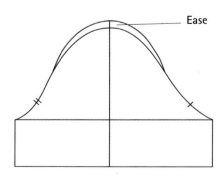

Ease

FIG. 23

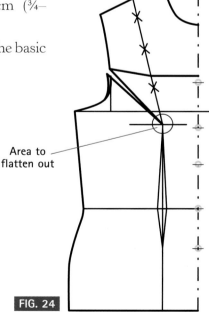

Area to flatten out

FIG. 24

29

THE BODICE

Facing for a closed collar

When the front of a garment is fastened using buttons, add a button stand to the right of the centre front line. The width of the button stand will depend on the style or the diameter of the buttons, but it is normally 2cm (¾in.).

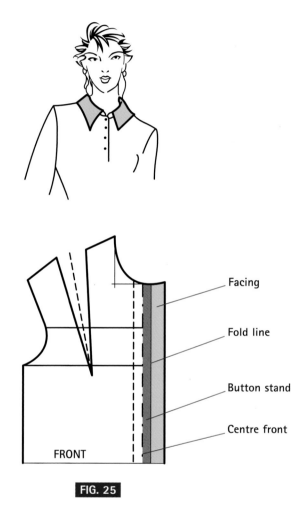

FIG. 25

Add a facing to the right of the button stand that will make the inside neat and tidy. Normally, the facing is 1–2cm (⅜–¾in.) wider than the button stand.

For the top of the facing, trace the neckline and invert it starting from the fold (the line between the button stand and the facing).

Facing for an open-neck collar

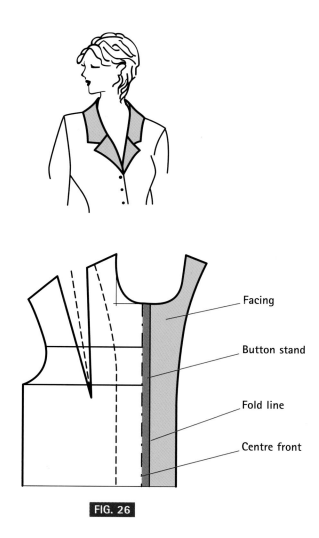

Facing

Button stand

Fold line

Centre front

FIG. 26

The facing for the open collar forms the lapel, and must be drawn on to the basic bodice, starting from the shoulder line. Its width will be a minimum of 4cm (1⅝in.). Trace out the shape and invert it, starting from the break line.

The button stand measurement varies according to the style of garment although the minimum amount is 2cm (¾in.).

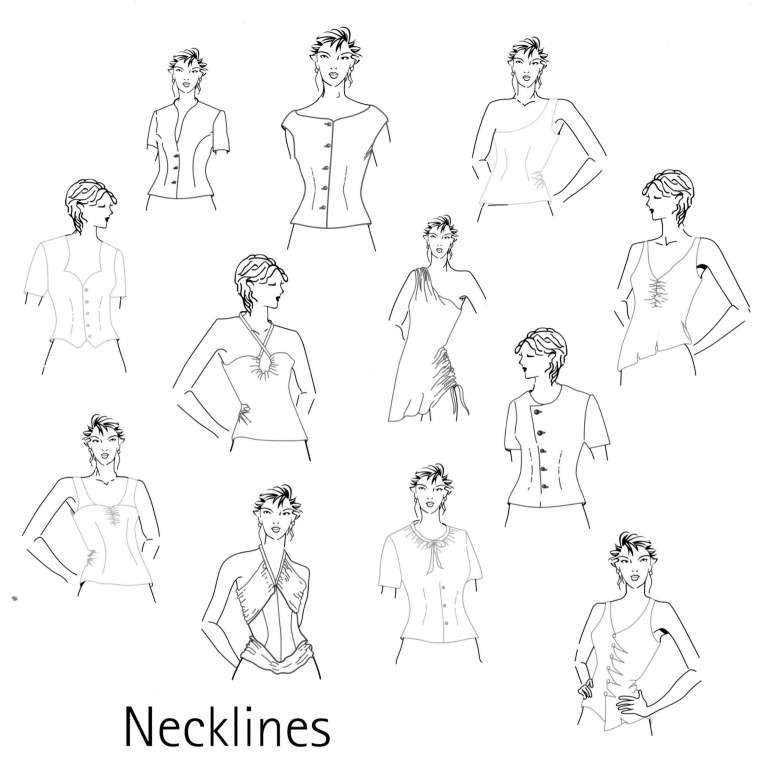

Necklines

A garment's neckline can determine its style. Each neckline will require changes to the styling and construction of the garment in relation to its design and the fabric used. Consideration must also be given to its finish – the neatening and facing.

Low boat neckline with buttoned front

First draw the bodice pattern and make the required alterations at the back (fig. 1) and front (fig. 2). For simplicity, draw the front neckline, then match it up to the back shoulder and draw the back neckline.

Trace off the neckline and armhole facings.

The front facing will be folded over to meet the neck facing, so shorten the length of the neck facing by the width of the front facing (see fig. 2).

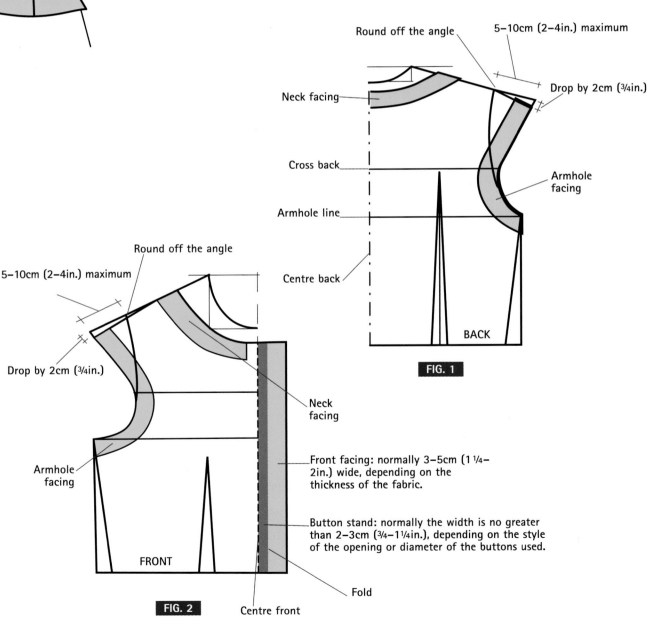

Round off the angle

5–10cm (2–4in.) maximum

Neck facing

Drop by 2cm (¾in.)

Cross back

Armhole facing

Armhole line

Centre back

BACK

FIG. 1

Round off the angle

5–10cm (2–4in.) maximum

Drop by 2cm (¾in.)

Neck facing

Armhole facing

Front facing: normally 3–5cm (1¼–2in.) wide, depending on the thickness of the fabric.

Button stand: normally the width is no greater than 2–3cm (¾–1¼in.), depending on the style of the opening or diameter of the buttons used.

FRONT

Fold

FIG. 2   Centre front

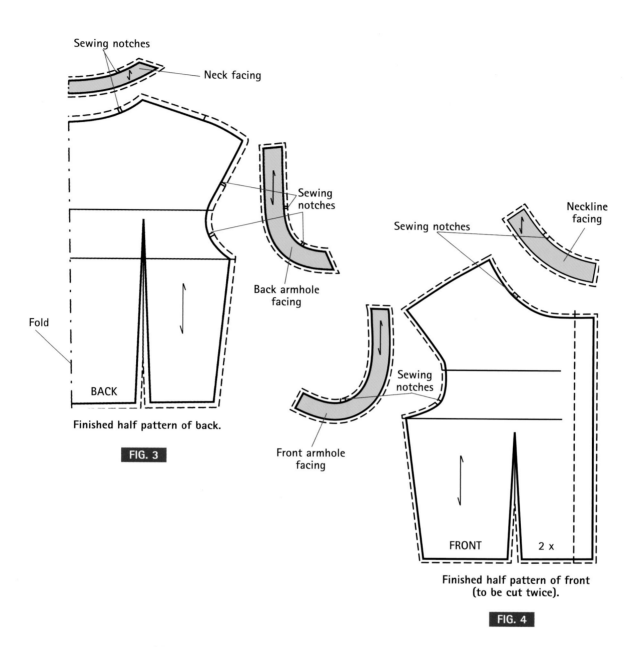

Sewing notches

Neck facing

Sewing notches

Back armhole facing

Fold

BACK

Finished half pattern of back.

FIG. 3

Sewing notches

Neckline facing

Front armhole facing

Sewing notches

FRONT

2 x

Finished half pattern of front (to be cut twice).

FIG. 4

For this style, lengthen the shoulder line by no more than 5–10cm (2–4in.), and to make the shape more aesthetically pleasing, drop it by 2cm (¾in.), rounding off the small angle created during construction (figs 1 and 2).

The front facing should always be 1cm (⅜in.) wider than the button stand, so that the facing overlaps the centre front line when it is folded back (fig. 2).

To prevent the bottom edge of a cap sleeve from stretching, cut the armhole facing on the straight grain (figs 3 and 4). Alternatively, reinforce the armhole facing by applying stay tape when sewing the garment.

Add a 1cm (⅜in.) seam allowance all around the finished pattern pieces.

Do not forget to mark the balance and sewing notches.

Asymmetrical low neckline, with buttoned front

Draft the bodice block using the given measurements, then make the pattern modifications. Draw the front and back bodice blocks with the basic neckline, lowering it at the front by 2–4cm (¾–1½ in.).

Make two half patterns of the two front sides (left and right) because the front is asymmetrical (the top part of the button fastening is not in the centre).

Mark the facing of the front right side following one of the two options shown in figs 3 and 4. The best option will depend on the style and type of fabric.

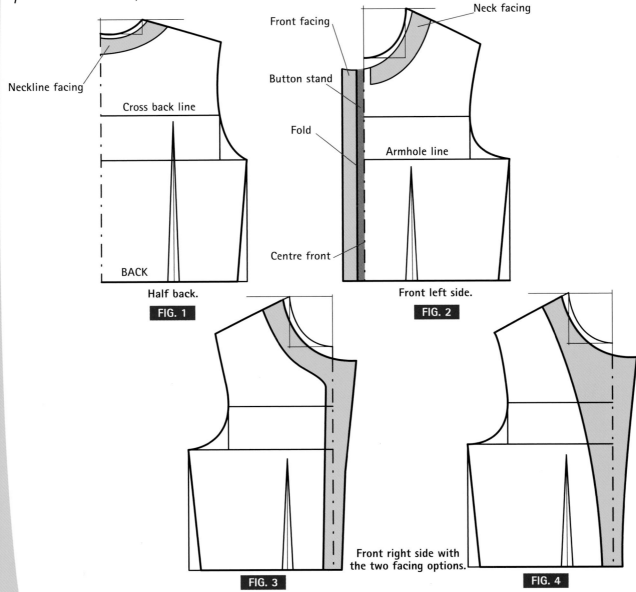

Neckline facing

Cross back line

BACK

Half back.
FIG. 1

Front facing

Neck facing

Button stand

Fold

Armhole line

Centre front

Front left side.
FIG. 2

FIG. 3

Front right side with the two facing options.

FIG. 4

36

The length of the neckline facing on the front left side is shorter than the neck measurement, to allow for the width of the front facing return.

The width of the front facing is normally a minimum of 3–5cm (1¼–2in.), depending on the thickness of the fabric.

The width of the button stand is normally no larger than 2–3cm (¾–1¼ in.), depending on the style of the button and its diameter.

The facing width is always 1cm (⅜in.) larger than the button stand width, so that the facing extends beyond the centre front line after it has been folded back.

Trace off all the facings.

Add a 1cm (⅜in.) seam allowance all around the finished pattern pieces.

Don't forget to mark the balance and sewing notches.

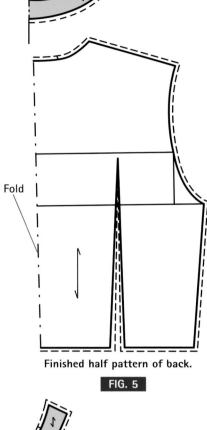

Fold

Finished half pattern of back.

FIG. 5

37

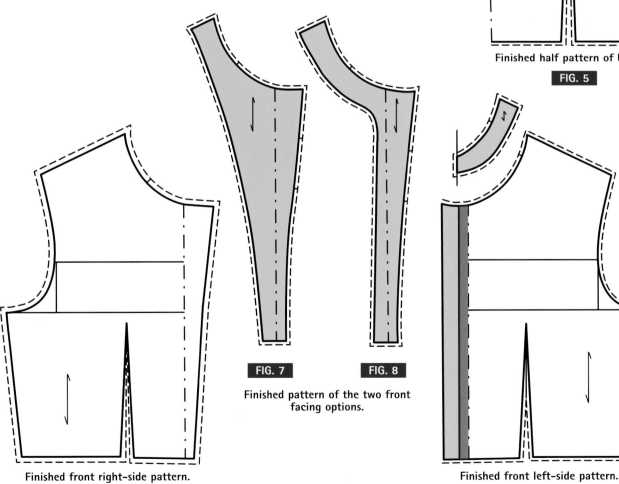

FIG. 7

FIG. 8

Finished pattern of the two front facing options.

Finished front right-side pattern.

FIG. 6

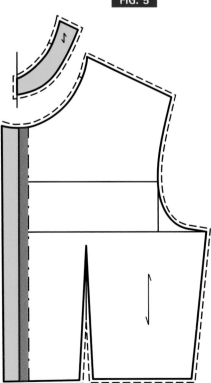

Finished front left-side pattern.

FIG. 9

NECKLINES

Straight plunge neckline, with buttoned front

Draft the bodice block using the given measurements, then apply the pattern modifications (figs 1 and 2). Make the armhole darts on the back and front without forgetting to adjust the two dart lines and smooth the angles formed during the construction.

For aesthetic and technical reasons, position the armhole dart on the cross back line or slightly above, but never below!

Due to the front neckline being very narrow and deep, only mark the button stand underneath the bust line (fig. 2) with a width of 3–5cm (1¼–2in.) according to the button diameter.

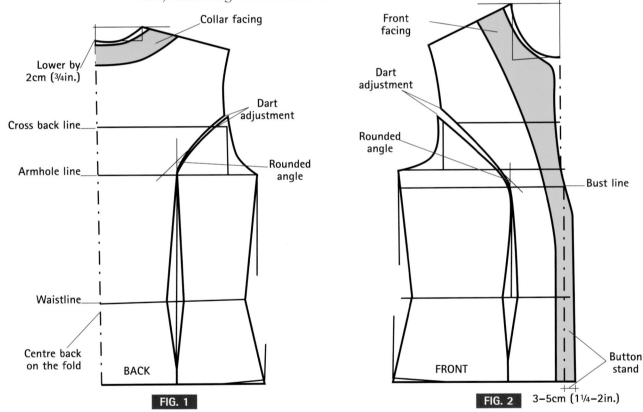

FIG. 1   BACK

FIG. 2   FRONT   3–5cm (1¼–2in.)

Lower the neckline by 2cm (¾in.) all around following the base line.

To obtain a finished half pattern, separate the two back parts and the two front parts.

Trace off the facings of the neckline and front. Finish the bottom of the front and back with a separate facing or a simple 2cm (¾in.) hem (measurement to be added to the pattern).

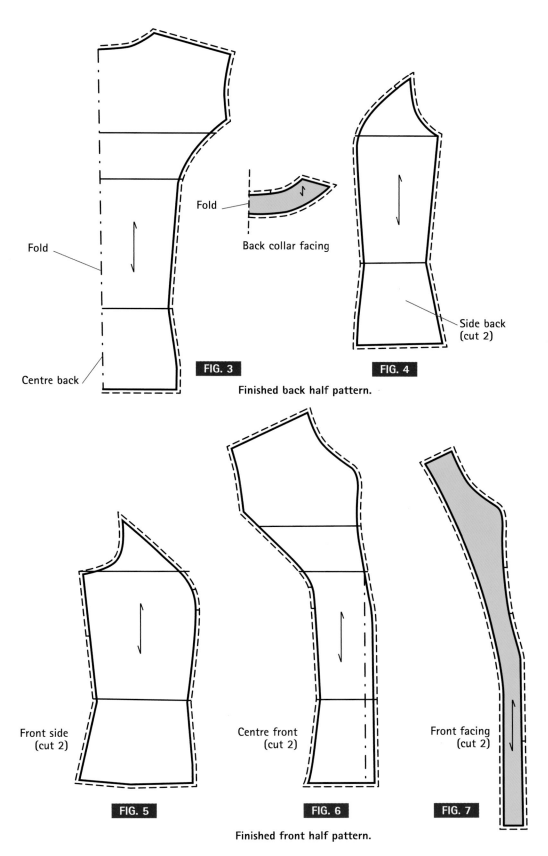

Fold

Fold

Back collar facing

FIG. 3

Centre back

Side back
(cut 2)

FIG. 4

Finished back half pattern.

Front side
(cut 2)

Centre front
(cut 2)

Front facing
(cut 2)

FIG. 5

FIG. 6

FIG. 7

Finished front half pattern.

Add a 1cm (⅜in.) seam all around the finished pattern pieces. The finished pattern of this model consists of many pieces, which can be confusing at the assembling stage, so do not to forget to add the balance and sewing notches.

NECKLINES

Round gathered neckline

The style shown here has a collar dart, which gives enough width for the gathers (fig. 2). To make it, first of all draw a basic block with a shoulder dart, then close it and transfer it to the neckline (see p.24, Dart manipulation).

Retrace the pattern onto another sheet of paper (fig. 3).

If the width of the collar does not seem large enough, and if you want to increase the number of gathers at the collar, slash it open to enlarge (fig. 3).

40

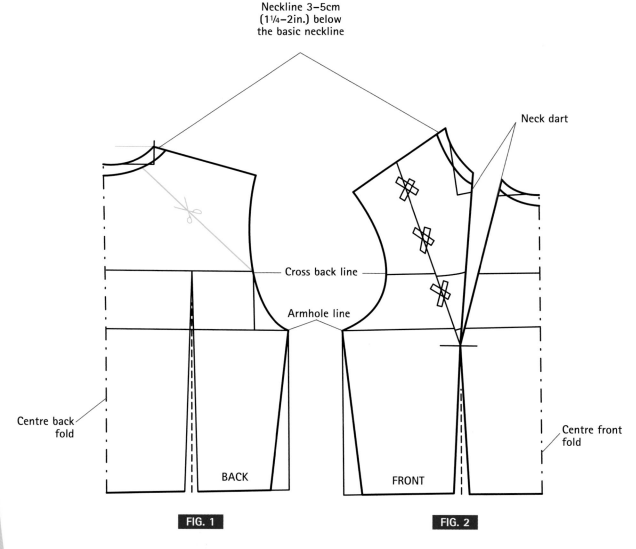

Neckline 3–5cm
(1¼–2in.) below
the basic neckline

Neck dart

Cross back line

Armhole line

Centre back
fold

Centre front
fold

BACK

FRONT

FIG. 1

FIG. 2

On the resulting pattern, draw the cutting line starting from the cross back line at the armhole, up to the middle of the neckline (fig. 3).

In order to keep the same armhole proportions, do not detach the cut sections. Spread the pieces to add the desired width (fig. 4) and retrace the pattern.

Make the back without gathers, finishing the neckline by including it into the bias binding.

Add a 1cm (⅜in.) seam allowance.

Mark the balance and sewing notches.

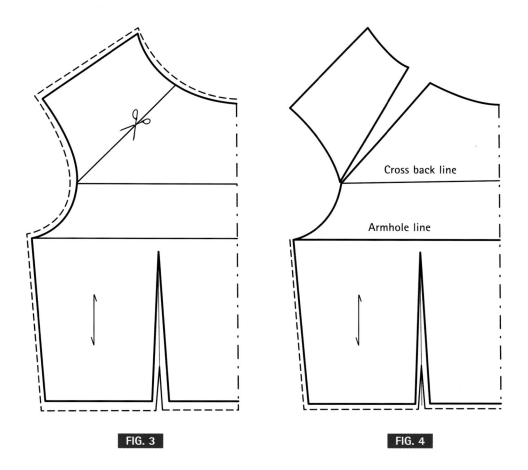

FIG. 3

FIG. 4

Variation on the back

To add gathers onto the back neckline of this style, follow the same method as for the front: draw a cutting line, as shown in fig. 1, starting from the armhole line, through the cross back line, up to the centre of the neckline. Cut and open up the two pieces to the desired width then retrace the back pattern.

Square neck with straps and gathers on the bust

Draft the basic bodice from the given measurements then mark the modification lines: the neckline and straps (figs 1 and 2).

If you do not want the facing to be gathered for the sake of comfort, then make this separately.

Mark the slash lines (fig. 2) where the gathers will be (see pp.59 and 63 for slashing technique).

Trace off the straps and the facings.

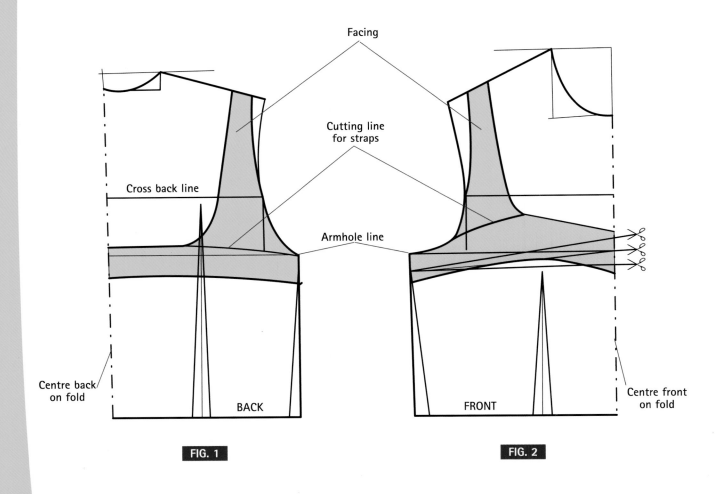

Facing

Cutting line
for straps

Cross back line

Armhole line

Centre back
on fold

BACK

Centre front
on fold

FRONT

FIG. 1

FIG. 2

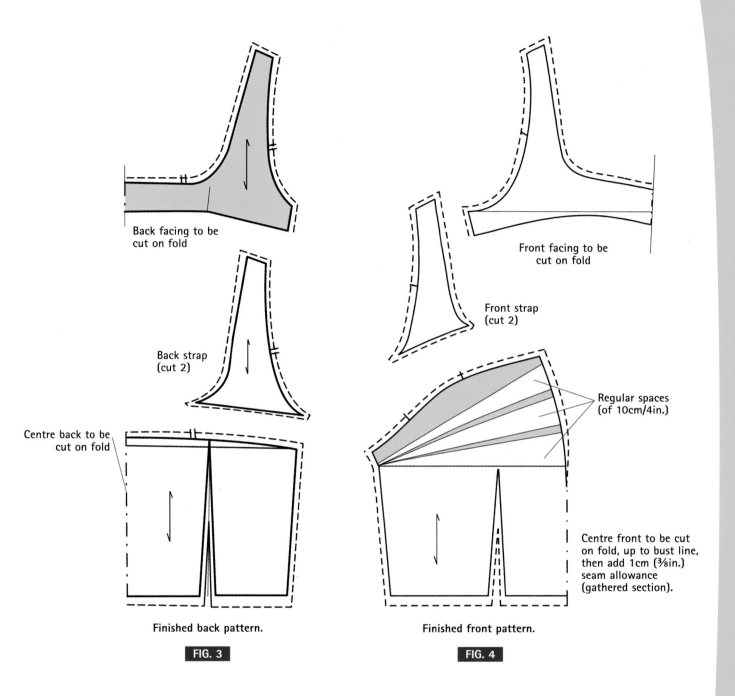

Back facing to be
cut on fold

Front facing to be
cut on fold

Back strap
(cut 2)

Front strap
(cut 2)

Centre back to be
cut on fold

Regular spaces
(of 10cm/4in.)

Centre front to be cut
on fold, up to bust line,
then add 1cm (⅜in.)
seam allowance
(gathered section).

Finished back pattern.

Finished front pattern.

FIG. 3

FIG. 4

43

Separate the straps from the rest of the back and front, adding a 1cm (⅜in.)
seam allowance all the way around (figs 3 and 4).

Evenly space out the sections cut from the front, then re-draw the pattern
(fig.4).

Add a 1cm (⅜in.) seam allowance.

Do not forget to mark the sewing notches, which are very important with
this style, so that the straps are assembled in the correct position.

NECKLINES

Asymmetrical neckline
with one strap

To achieve this style, make the modifications on the whole basic pattern (and not on the half pattern), because the bodice is one-shouldered and the neckline is asymmetrical.

Decide on the neckline shape, then draw the facings onto the whole pattern, both back and front (figs 1 and 2).

Trace off the front and back facings (figs 3 and 4).

The width of the facing underneath the armhole should be a minimum of 5cm (2in.) so that it does not move (it will be sewn into the side seam which will hold it in position).

If possible, draw the inner edge of the facing on the bias so that the fabric can stretch.

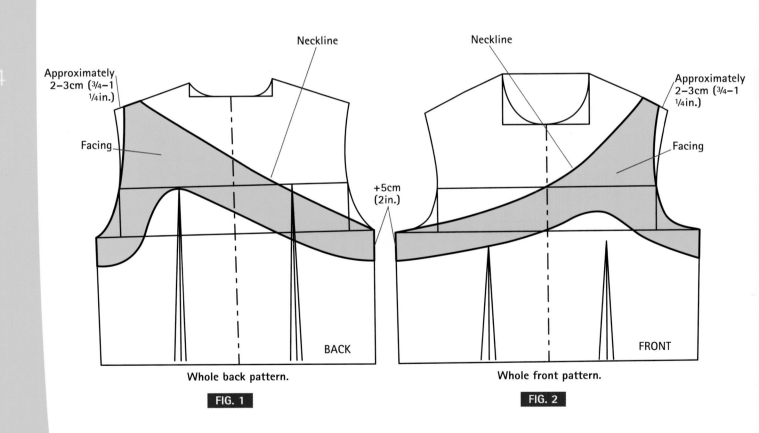

Whole back pattern.

FIG. 1

Whole front pattern.

FIG. 2

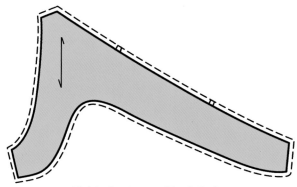

Finished pattern of back facing.

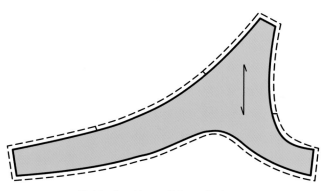

Finished pattern of front facing.

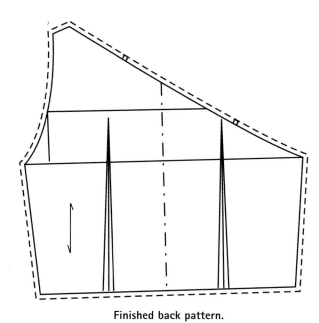

Finished back pattern.

FIG. 3

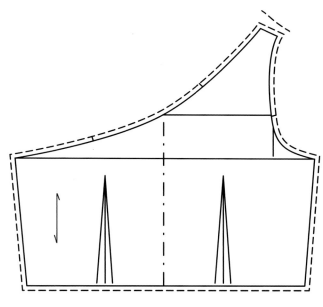

Finished front pattern.

FIG. 4

When assembling the garment add a stay tape to prevent the front and back neckline from gaping.

Add a 1cm (⅜in.) seam allowance all around the finished pattern pieces.

Don't forget to mark the balance and sewing notches.

Heart-shaped neckline with buttoned front

Draft the basic block using the given measurements, then add the front and back pattern modifications.

Draw the front and back facings, then trace them off.

The hem facing will need to be fixed with small stitches, so that it does not drop.

To reinforce the rounded parts of the neckline, use a fusible interlining, and add a stay tape when assembling to prevent gaping.

46

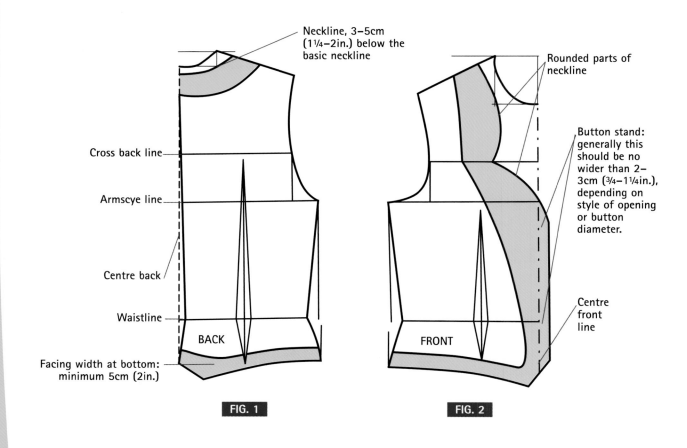

Neckline, 3–5cm (1¼–2in.) below the basic neckline

Cross back line

Armscye line

Centre back

Waistline

Facing width at bottom: minimum 5cm (2in.)

BACK

FIG. 1

Rounded parts of neckline

Button stand: generally this should be no wider than 2–3cm (¾–1¼in.), depending on style of opening or button diameter.

Centre front line

FRONT

FIG. 2

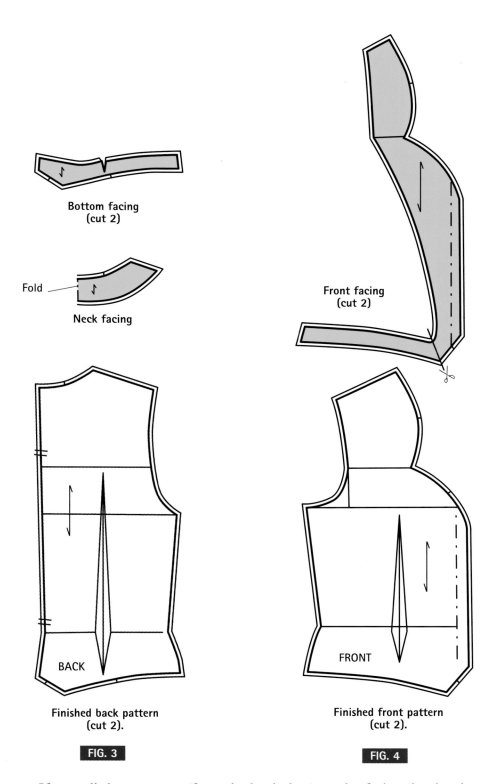

Bottom facing
(cut 2)

Fold

Neck facing

Front facing
(cut 2)

47

BACK

FRONT

Finished back pattern
(cut 2).

Finished front pattern
(cut 2).

FIG. 3

FIG. 4

If a small dart appears (from the back dart) on the facing that has been traced off from the pattern, it must be kept, however small, so that the garment's facing fits perfectly.

Add a seam allowance of 1cm (⅜in.) all around the finished pattern pieces.

Do not forget to mark balance and sewing notches.

Make the front facing in one piece or, to save on fabric, divide in two as indicated in the diagram.

Halter neck with gathered keyhole

Style 8

Draft the bodice block, using the given measurements, then apply the pattern modifications.

On the back armhole line draw the back facing using a minimum width of 5–7cm (2–2¾in.), then trace it off.

Mark the height (e.g. 15–17cm/6–6¾in.) and the keyhole shape of the neckline.

Draw the front facing (fig. 2, in yellow) then trace it off.

For the gathered part enlarge the 'keyhole' by drawing the slashing lines shown in fig. 2.

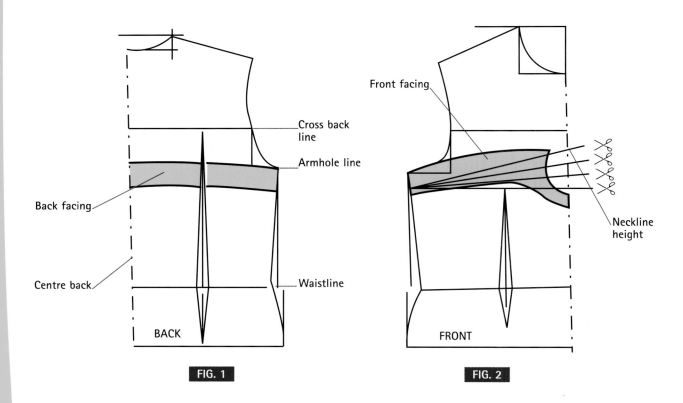

Cross back line

Armhole line

Back facing

Centre back

Waistline

BACK

FIG. 1

Front facing

Neckline height

FRONT

FIG. 2

The small back dart must be included in the back facing as well (no. 1). Alternatively, close the dart on the pattern then re-draw the facing – this is the best solution to maintain the length and pattern shape (no. 2).

Evenly space out the slashed sections of the front to the desired width, then re-draw the pattern (fig. 4).

Make a 'tunnel' to slip the halter neck strap through by cutting out a strip the same shape as the neckline (fig. 4). Gather up the fabric as in fig. 2 and add the strip of facing. This method ensures that the keyhole gathers will not move, as they are held in place by the inside facing (which is not gathered).

If you want the gathers to be moveable, re-trace the pattern after the sections have been spread out (fig. 5), re-draw the shape of the facing, and trace it off. Construct a 'tunnel' all around the neckline, with an opening of 1cm (⅜in.) in which to slide in the halter neck strap.

Add a 1cm (⅜in.) seam allowance.

Mark the balance and sewing notches.

49

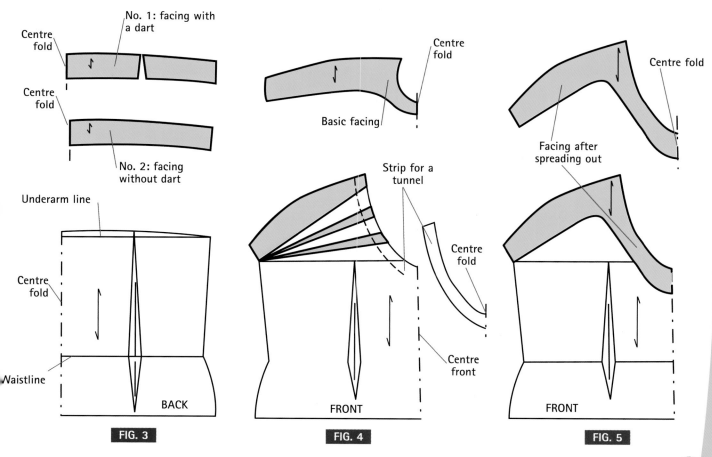

FIG. 3   FIG. 4   FIG. 5

NECKLINES

V-neck halter top

First make the block using the given measurements, then apply the pattern modifications to the back (fig. 1) and front (fig. 2).

To simplify the work, replace the back facing with a hem of 5–7cm (2–2¾in.) minimum, folded inside. In this case, cut out the back neckline in a straight line. This normally follows the armhole line. Add the hem width onto this line.

Draw the seam lines that will delineate the flat or non-gathered section of the bodice, then draw the slashing lines (at regular intervals) on the top and bottom sections of the bodice. These lines will serve as indicators for spacing out the gathers.

50

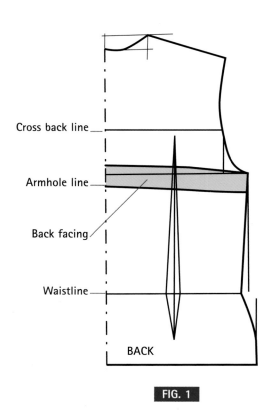

Cross back line

Armhole line

Back facing

Waistline

BACK

FIG. 1

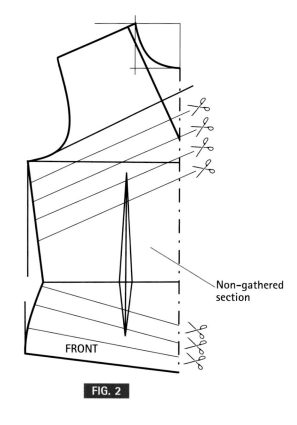

Non-gathered section

FRONT

FIG. 2

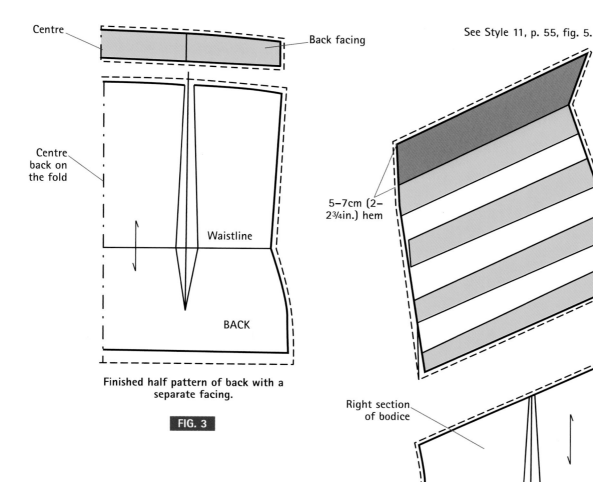

Centre

Back facing

Centre back on the fold

Waistline

BACK

Finished half pattern of back with a separate facing.

FIG. 3

See Style 11, p. 55, fig. 5.

5–7cm (2–2¾in.) hem

Right section of bodice

Waistline

Centre front on the fold

5–7cm (2–2¾in.) hem

Separate the top and bottom gathered sections of the front from the flat middle section (fig. 4), so that the seams can be used to carefully mark the volume of the gathers. Alternatively, this style can be cut as a single piece (without separating the sections), which will mean that the joins between the flat and gathered sections will be more fluid.

Evenly space out the cut sections (here 5cm/2in.). Increase the spacing for more gathers and reduce it for less.

To avoid making the facings at the top or the bottom of the front bodice, draw on a 5–7cm (2–2¾in.) wide hem.

Re-draw the finished pattern and add the 1cm (½in.) seam line.

Don't forget to add the balance and sewing notches.

Finished half pattern of front.

FIG. 4

51

Sleeveless v-necked 'waistcoat', buttoned on one side

First make the block using the given measurements, then apply the pattern modifications to the front and back.

On the back block draw the facings of the neckline, armhole and the bottom of the bodice, then trace them off (fig. 1).

As the front of this style is asymmetrical, draw both the front left and right blocks so that the pattern modifications can be applied separately to each side.

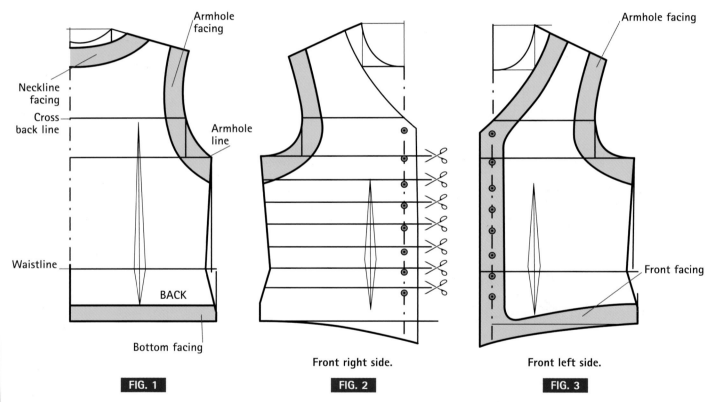

Armhole facing

Neckline facing

Cross back line

Armhole line

Waistline

BACK

Bottom facing

FIG. 1

Front right side.

FIG. 2

Armhole facing

Front facing

Front left side.

FIG. 3

For the front left side, mark the height and the shape of the neckline as well as the shape of the waistcoat points on the bottom, then add the button stand measurement (2cm/¾in. minimum). Draw the armhole and front facings, then trace them off (fig. 3).

For the front right side, reverse the left side and copy. Mark the button positions as these will help establish the cutting lines, each fold being held in position by a button (fig. 2). Draw the slash lines.

Cut the facing of the front left side in one single piece. Or, if necessary to economise on fabric, in two parts, at an angle (see fig. 5).

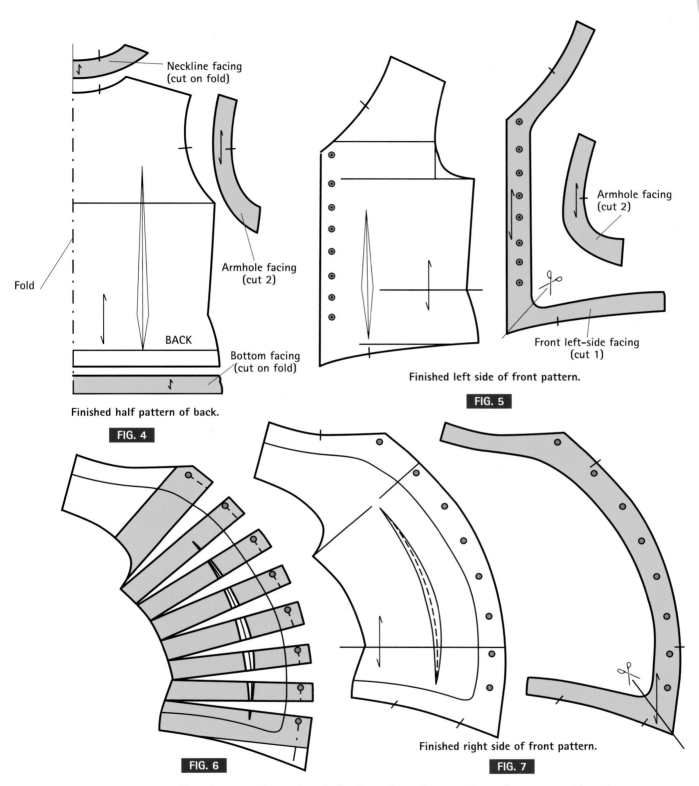

Neckline facing
(cut on fold)

Armhole facing
(cut 2)

Fold

BACK

Bottom facing
(cut on fold)

Finished half pattern of back.

FIG. 4

Armhole facing
(cut 2)

Front left-side facing
(cut 1)

Finished left side of front pattern.

FIG. 5

FIG. 6

Finished right side of front pattern.

FIG. 7

53

Evenly spread out the slashed sections then re-draw the pattern (fig. 6).
Trace off the facing from this pattern (fig. 7).

Draw a 1cm (⅜in.) seam allowance all around the finished pattern pieces.
Do not forget to mark on balance and sewing notches.

Sleeveless v-shaped neckline, gathered at the bust

Style 11

Draft the basic block using the given measurements, then apply the pattern modifications onto the back and front as shown in figs 1 and 2.

Draw the slashing lines for the centre front gathers.

Trace off the back and front facings.

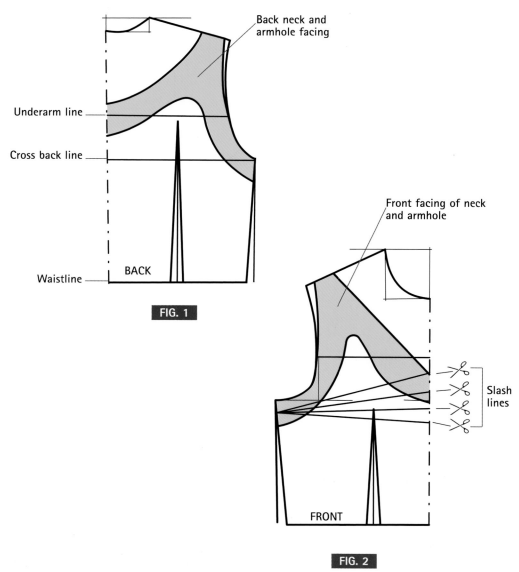

Back neck and armhole facing

Underarm line

Cross back line

Waistline   BACK

FIG. 1

Front facing of neck and armhole

Slash lines

FRONT

FIG. 2

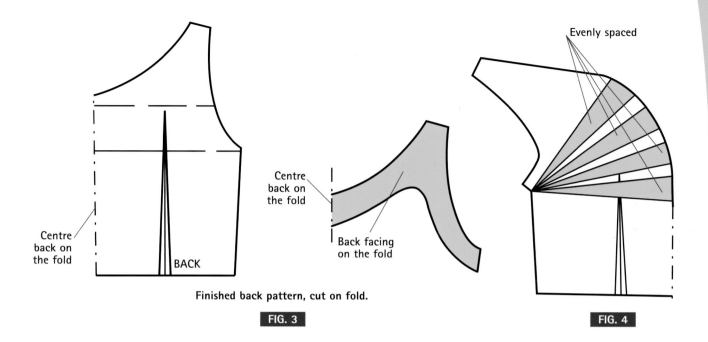

Centre
back on
the fold

BACK

Finished back pattern, cut on fold.

FIG. 3

Centre
back on
the fold

Back facing
on the fold

Evenly spaced

FIG. 4

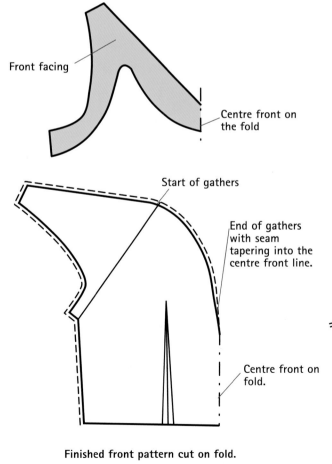

Front facing

Centre front on
the fold

Start of gathers

End of gathers
with seam
tapering into the
centre front line.

Centre front on
fold.

Finished front pattern cut on fold.

FIG. 5

Evenly spread the slashed sections, then trace off the front pattern (fig. 4).

Do not forget to place the notches at the start and end of the gathered section.

The bottom of the bodice for this style is asymmetrical; unfold the back and front patterns to give the shape at the bottom (see fig. 6).

To avoid points in the side seams, draw a straight line 2–3cm (¾–1¼in.) long at each end of the diagonal line at the bottom of the bodice.

Add a 1cm seam allowance all around the finished pattern.

Don't forget to add plenty of notches.

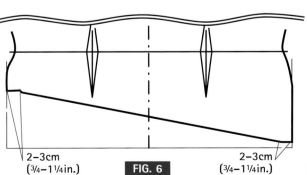

2–3cm
(¾–1¼in.)

2–3cm
(¾–1¼in.)

FIG. 6

55

NECKLINES

Asymmetrical neckline, with gathered strap

Style 12

Draft the basic block using the given measurements, then apply the pattern modifications onto the back and front as shown in figs 1 and 2.

As the style here is asymmetrical (the bodice being held in place by a single strap) make the complete front and back patterns (figs 1 and 2).

To construct the facings refer to Style 6 (see p.44) but remember that with this style the front facing must line the gathered fabric on the shoulder, so it needs to be deep enough without flattening the bust.

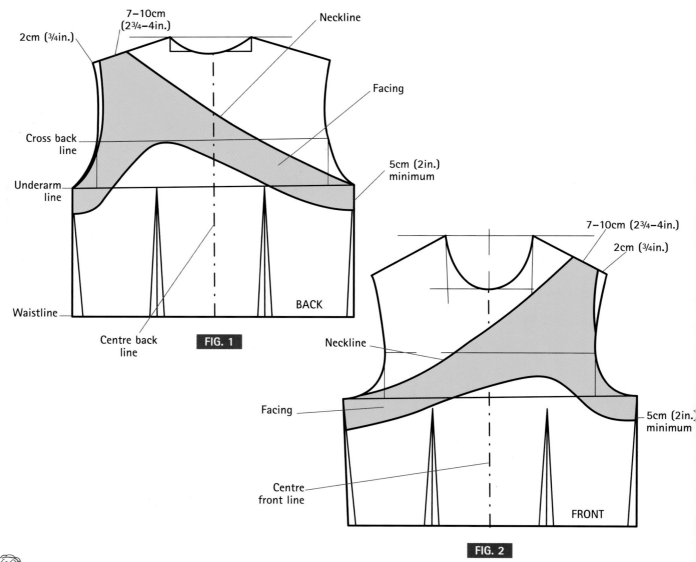

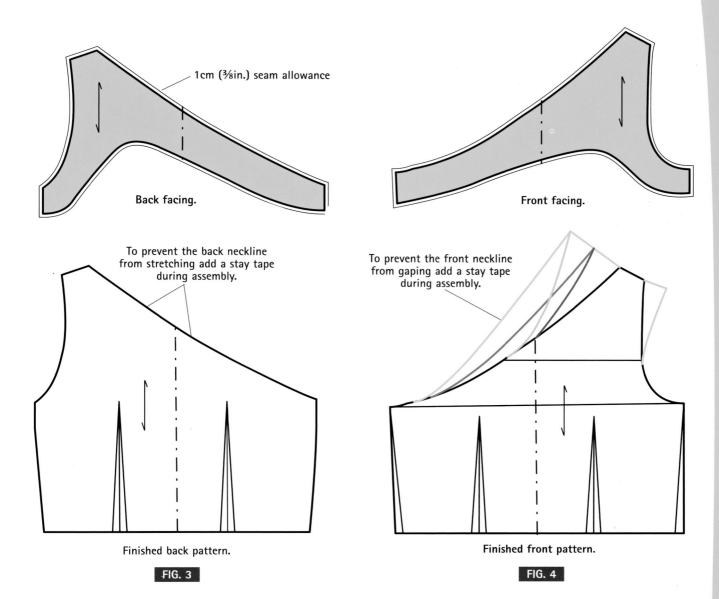

1cm (⅜in.) seam allowance

Back facing.

Front facing.

To prevent the back neckline from stretching add a stay tape during assembly.

To prevent the front neckline from gaping add a stay tape during assembly.

Finished back pattern.

FIG. 3

Finished front pattern.

FIG. 4

To obtain the finished front pattern, trace off the whole or part of the neckline, (fig. 4) as well as the armhole curve from the cross front line.

The four colours shown in fig. 4 represent the four possible gather styles: the yellow line will create longer folds with voluminous gathers, the blue creates long folds with smaller gathers, the green creates short folds with voluminous gathers, and the red creates short folds with smaller gathers.

Draw a 1cm (⅜in.) seam allowance all around the finished pattern pieces.

Do not forget to mark on balance and sewing notches.

NECKLINES

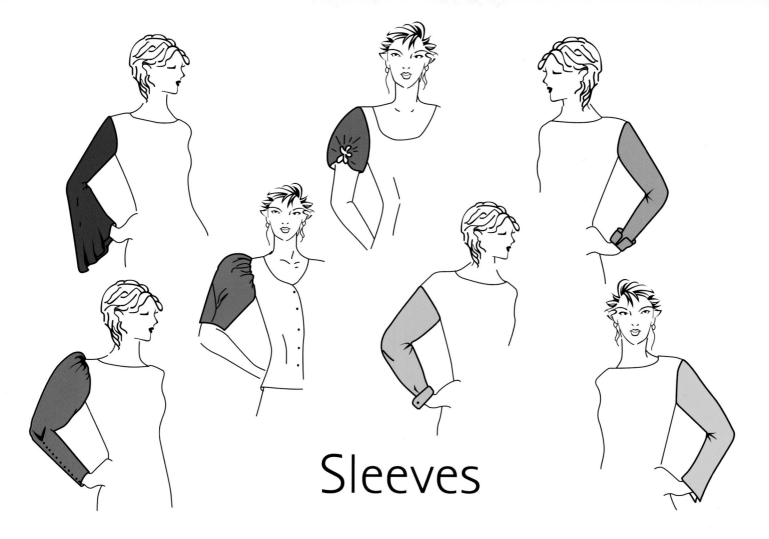

Sleeves

Sleeves are essential features that can define the style and look of a garment.

They are generally divided into two groups: short sleeves and long sleeves. Even though the two categories follow the same drafting principles, the rules for making the finished patterns are very different; this is why the two groups are discussed separately here.

A variety of styles have been chosen in order to illustrate the construction and structure needed. The method used here to obtain a sleeve pattern is that of slashing (cutting), which is very easy.

Once mastered, this simple and effective technique will allow you to make your own, more elaborate, patterns.

Showing the construction steps individually allows for more creativity. There is scope to develop and personalise each style to the point where a new design can be created in the same style by applying another construction process.

Construction of the basic sleeve block

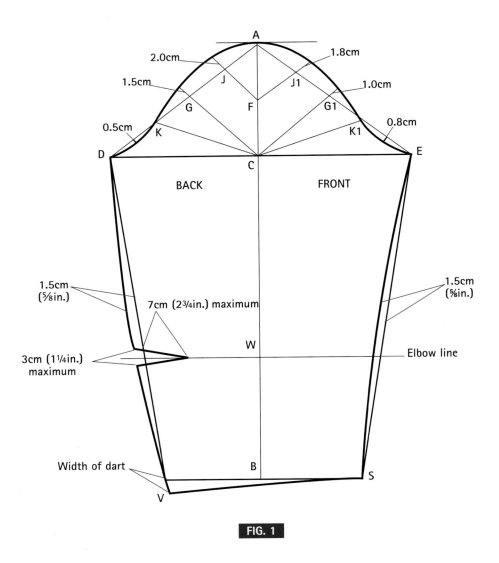

A

2.0cm

1.8cm

1.5cm

1.0cm

J   J1

G   F   G1

0.5cm

0.8cm

K   K1

D   C   E

BACK   FRONT

1.5cm
(⅝in.)

1.5cm
(⅝in.)

7cm (2¾in.) maximum

W

Elbow line

3cm (1¼in.)
maximum

Width of dart

B

S

V

FIG. 1

The construction of the basic sleeve block is based on the length and depth of the armhole (see following page).

The following example shows the measurements used in constructing the basic sleeve.
– Length of sleeve = 58cm
– Depth of armhole = 19cm
– Length of front armhole = 21cm
– Length of back armhole = 21.4cm

1. Length of sleeve, AB = 58cm.

2. AC is the depth of the armhole minus one fifth of the depth of the armhole, or 19cm – (19cm ÷ 5) = 15.2cm.

3. CE is three-quarters of the length of the front armhole, or (21cm x 3) ÷ 4 = 15.75cm.

4. CD is three-quarters of the length of the back armhole, or (21.4cm x 3) ÷ 4 = 16.05cm.

5. Join AD and AE.

6. From F, draw two straight lines JF and J1F, at an angle of 45° with AC. From C, draw two straight lines GC and G1C, at an angle of 45° with AC.

7. DK is half of DG, EK1 is half of EG1. Draw the head of the sleeve with a French curve or a Patternmaster.

8. The height of the elbow is AW, or 35.5cm; the width of the dart is 3cm (1⅛in.) maximum; the length of the dart is 7cm (2¾in.) maximum.

9. Join DV + width of dart.

Whatever style is required, it is essential to construct a basic sleeve block according to the length and depth of the bodice armhole.

The steps of construction must be carried out in the following order:
1. Draft the basic bodice block
2. Make alterations and adjustments
3. Measure the length and depth of the armhole (see p.62)
4. Draft the sleeve pattern from these measurements.

Depth and length (or circumference) of the armhole

The basic sleeve pattern is drafted from the measurements of the depth and length of the armhole. This gives a well-adjusted head to the sleeve. This method of construction is useful as it allows for the making of alterations necessary to create different styles.

The method to obtain the measurements for the depth and length of the armhole is shown in fig. 1.

1. Place the back and front bodice blocks side by side (fig. 1).

2. Join points A and B.

3. Extend the side line up to meet AB.

4. The measurement XY gives the depth of the armhole.

5. The length of the armhole is measured with a tape measure placed around the circumference of the armhole from the shoulder to the side line. It is best to measure the back armhole length and the front armhole length separately.

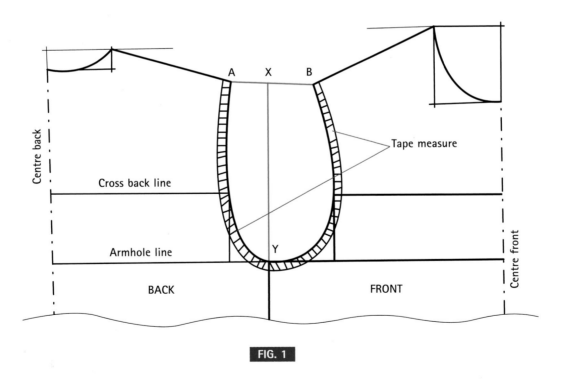

FIG. 1

Making a sleeve pattern by slashing

Any style can be developed from the basic sleeve block. Slashing is the simplest technique.

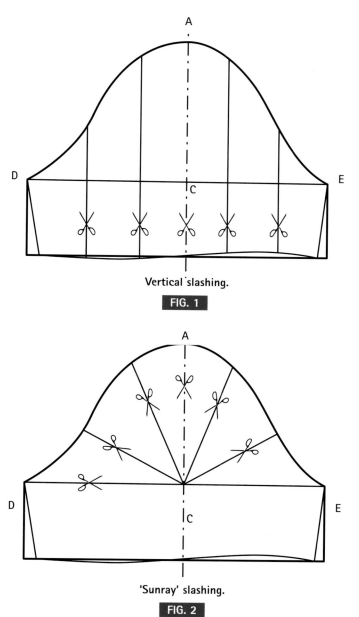

Vertical slashing.

FIG. 1

'Sunray' slashing.

FIG. 2

Don't forget!
Whichever technique used, slashing vertically or in rays, the cut parts must be separated at regular intervals, keeping the centre sleeve line vertical in order to keep the shape of the sleeve and its proportions.

63

Short sleeves

The short sleeve styles shown here are examples of the slashing method and construction technique. The coloured parts of the diagrams show the different stages of drafting the sleeve.

The lengths of the sleeve are not always given, but when they are it is only as a guide, to enable you to personalise and adapt the style.

For clarity in the diagrams the seam allowances are not always shown but they must always be added.

Finally, remember that sewing notches are essential on the finished pattern and must not be forgotten.

Sleeve with gathered head

Draft the basic sleeve to the desired length, taking account of the length and depth of the armhole.

For this style, the height and width of the sleeve head need to be increased. To do this use 'sunray' slashing, which is the most suitable technique here: divide the sleeve head into equal pieces and number the parts to be cut (fig. 1).

Keep the centre line of the sleeve vertical.

Spread out the cut pieces at regular intervals, to obtain the desired fullness (fig. 2).

Re-draw the sleeve, removing all the angles formed during the spreading out.

Add a seam allowance of 1cm (⅜in.) to the finished pattern.

Add balance and sewing notches.

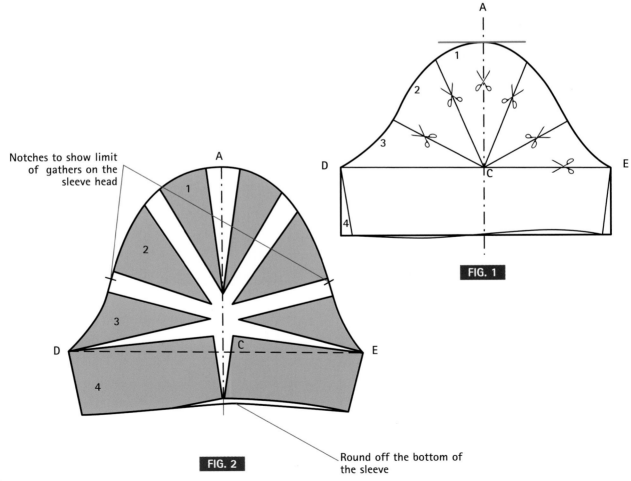

Notches to show limit of gathers on the sleeve head

Round off the bottom of the sleeve

FIG. 1

FIG. 2

Tulip sleeve without gathers

This style is made with two overlapping pieces.

First, draft the basic sleeve according to the length and depth of the armhole, with an ease of 3–4cm (1¼–1½in.) and a length of 24cm, for example.

Draw one of the two cutting lines for one of the two pieces of the sleeve. The other cutting line for the second part is symmetrical to the first (fig. 1). In general, these cutting lines start at the level of the cross back line (on the armhole).

Trace out the the back side and the front side of the sleeve separately (fig. 2).

Put in balance notches (one notch for the front and two notches for the back) as well as sewing notches.

Add a seam allowance of 1cm (⅜in.) to the finished pattern pieces for the two parts of the sleeve (back side and front side).

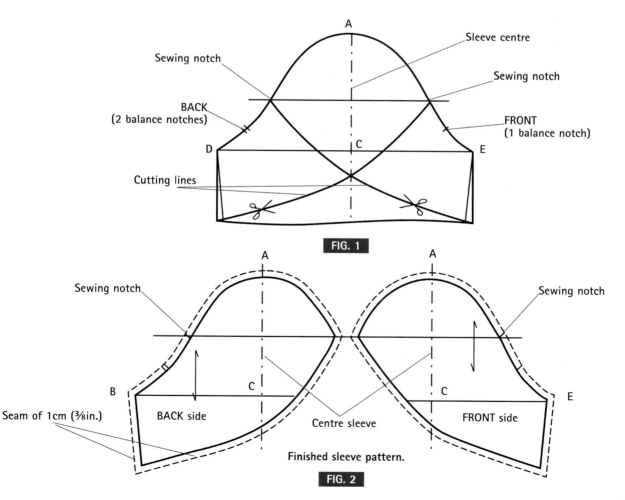

FIG. 1

FIG. 2

Finished sleeve pattern.

SLEEVES

67

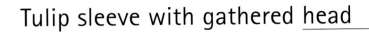

Tulip sleeve with gathered head

First, draft the basic sleeve according to the length and depth of the armhole, giving the sleeve a length of 24cm, for example. To give volume to the sleeve head with gathers, slash as shown in fig. 1.

Spread out the two top pieces, keeping the central line of the sleeve vertical, and re-draw the sleeve pattern (fig. 2).

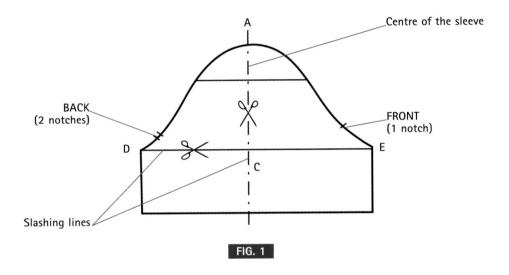

FIG. 1

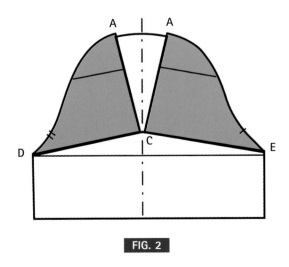

FIG. 2

Spreading the two pieces apart horizontally enables the required amount of gathers to be added at the sleeve head. Bringing the two pieces up vertically also allows the height at the crown to be increased. You will need to support the gathers with a tulle pad or a shoulder pad.

To finish the pattern (figs 3 and 4), follow the instructions for Style 2, tulip sleeve without gathers (see p. 67).

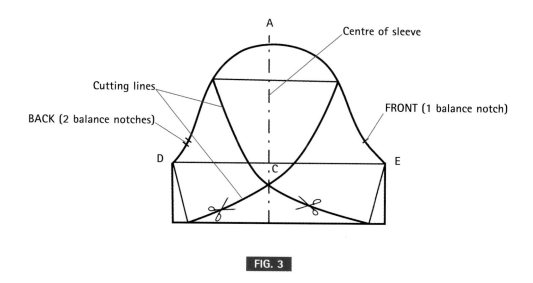

FIG. 3

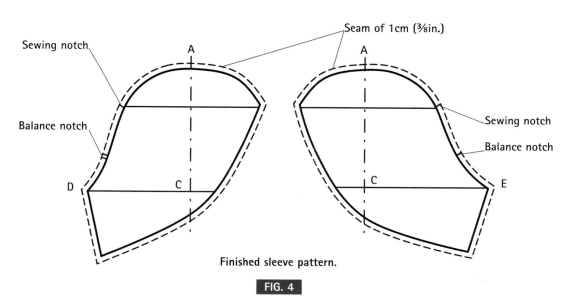

Finished sleeve pattern.

FIG. 4

69

SLEEVES

Sleeve with overlapping asymmetrical flounces

Construct the basic sleeve according to the length and depth of the armhole, with a sleeve length of about 25cm (10in.) (fig. 1).

Draw the two cutting lines (fig. 1) and trace off the two halves of the sleeve (fig. 2). Draw slash lines at regular intervals on each of these sleeve pieces (fig. 2).

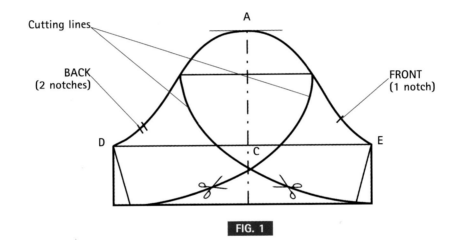

FIG. 1

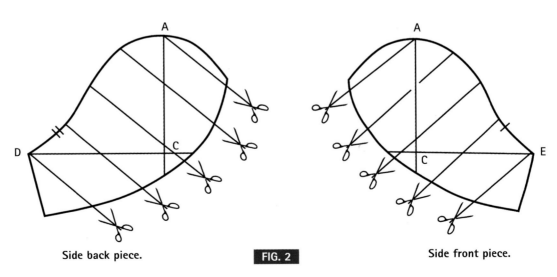

Side back piece.

FIG. 2

Side front piece.

PATTERN-DRAFTING FOR FASHION: THE BASICS

Slash without cutting through the head of the sleeve, to avoid distorting the shape of the armhole.

Spread out the cut pieces at regular intervals, keeping the central line of the sleeve vertical (fig. 3).

Re-draw the sleeve pattern (fig. 3).

Round off the angles formed after spreading out the cut pieces.

Don't forget to put in the balance and sewing notches, and add a 1cm (⅜in.) seam allowance to the finished pattern pieces.

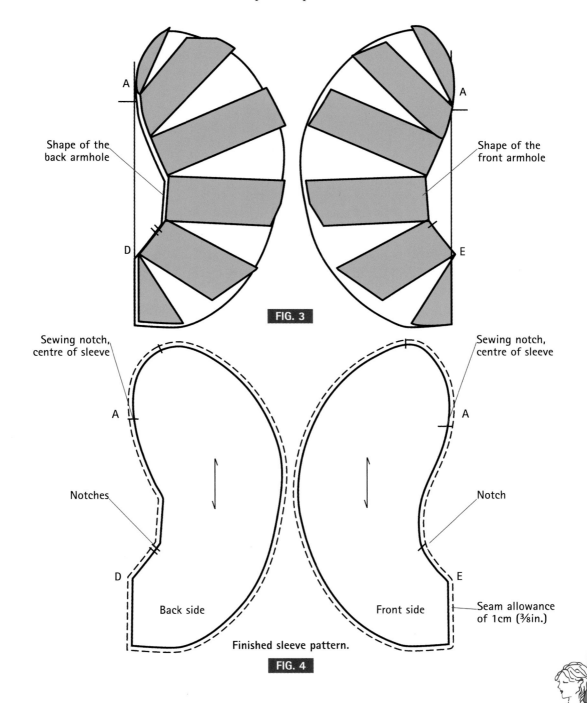

Shape of the back armhole

Shape of the front armhole

A

A

D

E

FIG. 3

Sewing notch, centre of sleeve

Sewing notch, centre of sleeve

A

A

Notches

Notch

D

E

Back side

Front side

Seam allowance of 1cm (⅜in.)

Finished sleeve pattern.

FIG. 4

Butterfly sleeve (or bell sleeve)

To construct this sleeve use the vertical slashing technique (see p. 63).

Draft the basic sleeve according to the length and depth of the armhole, with ease of 2cm (¾in.) and a maximum length of 25cm (10in.). Then draw the slash lines (fig. 1).

Spread out the cut pieces at regular intervals, keeping the central line of the sleeve vertical, then re-draw the pattern (fig. 2).

Do not detach the cut pieces, so as to keep the exact shape of the sleeve.

For a very flared sleeve the pieces need to be spread even more. Divide the basic sleeve pattern into more pieces (eight, ten or more) to help make it easier to draw the new pattern. For a sleeve that is only slightly flared, divide the pattern into two or four pieces only.

Put in balance and sewing notches, and add a seam allowance of 1cm (⅜in.) to the finished pattern.

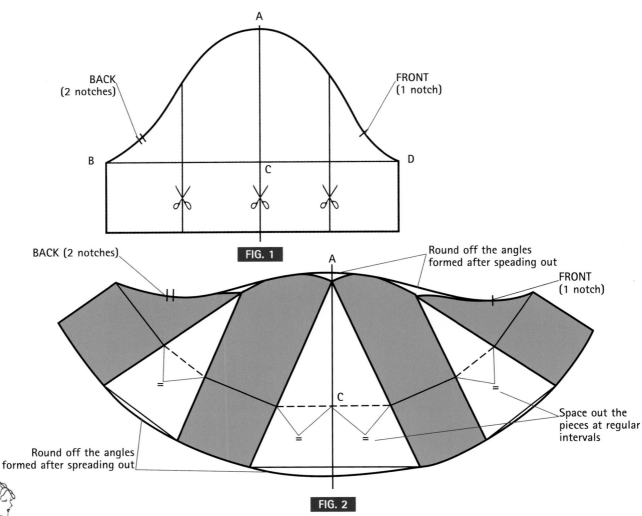

72

Sleeve gathered at the bottom

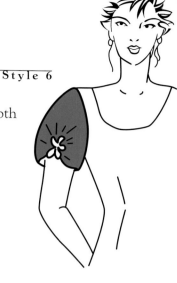

Start with the basic sleeve draft, depending on the length and depth of the armhole, giving the sleeve the desired length.

Mark the centre of the gathers, then draw the slash lines (fig. 1).

From the centre of the gathers, spread out the pieces at regular intervals, as shown in fig. 2.

To keep the shape of the sleeve, do not detach the cut pieces.

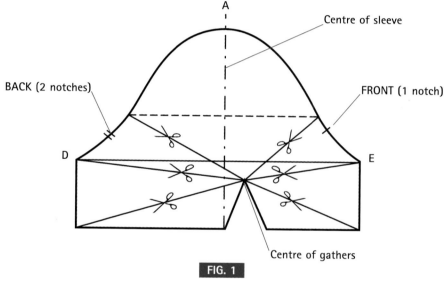

FIG. 1

73

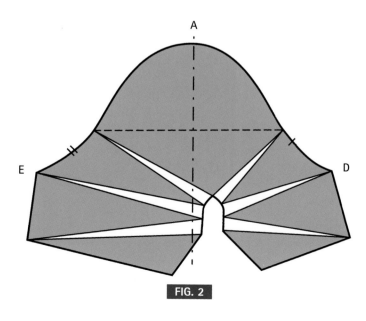

FIG. 2

SLEEVES

Sleeve with a gathered insert

For this sleeve style either use a fairly stiff fabric, or interline the part of the sleeve head to be gathered. Alternatively, a pad of gathered tulle can be inserted underneath the sleeve head.

First, draft the basic sleeve according to the length and depth of the armhole, and to the desired length.

Draw the slash lines (fig. 1) then trace off this part of the sleeve.

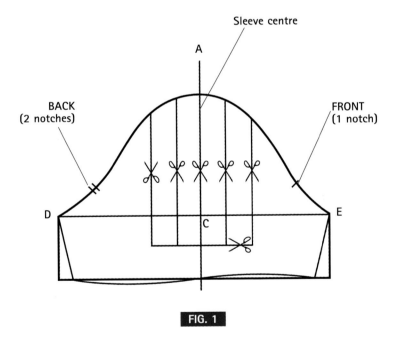

FIG. 1

74

Spread out the cut pieces horizontally, at regular intervals, keeping the centre line of the sleeve vertical (fig. 2).

Re-draw this part of the sleeve pattern raising the head of the sleeve by 3–5cm (1¼–2in.) to obtain the gathers. Rounding off the bottom of the sleeve by 2–3cm (¾–1¼in.) will also increase the volume (fig. 2).

Don't forget to add balance and sewing notches and a seam allowance of 1cm (⅜in.) all around the finished pattern.

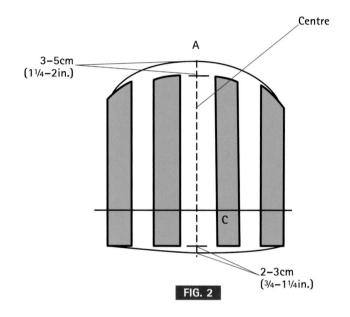

FIG. 2

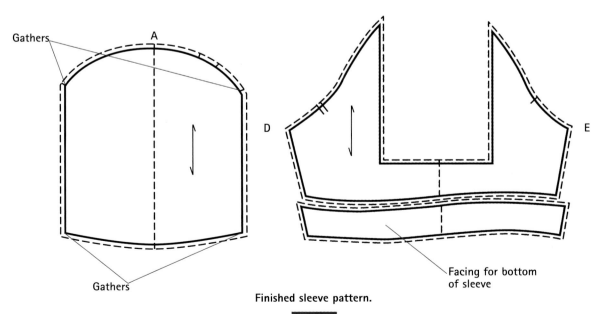

Finished sleeve pattern.

FIG. 3

Puffed sleeve with seam

Draft the basic sleeve pattern according to the length and depth of the armhole, giving the sleeve the desired length.

If the fabric to be used is very soft, proceed as for Style 7 (see p. 76). Support the volume at the head of the sleeve with a pad, or reinforce inside with a firmer fabric such as fine interlining or stiff tulle.

The volume of the sleeve depends on how much the cut pieces are spread out: the more they are spaced out, the fuller the sleeve.

Draw the slash lines as shown in fig. 1.

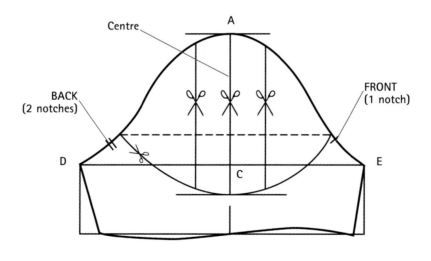

FIG. 1

The construction is always made in relation to the vertical line which is the centre of the sleeve.

Slash the fabric without detaching the pieces, to keep the exact shape and proportion.

Spread out the pieces, keeping the central line of the sleeve vertical (fig. 2).

Re-draw the sleeve pattern as shown in fig. 3.

Add notches and a seam allowance of 1cm (⅜in.) to the finished pattern.

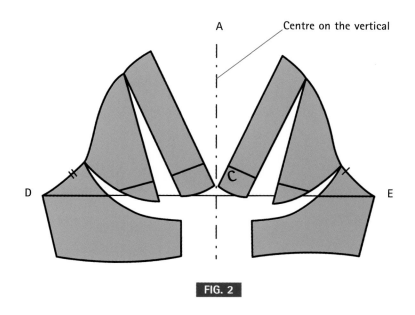

FIG. 2

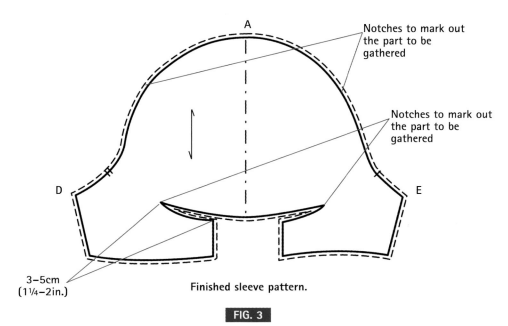

Finished sleeve pattern.

FIG. 3

SLEEVES

Lantern or Chinese lantern sleeve

This style is called 'lantern' or 'Chinese lantern' because of its shape. The long version can also have a very attractive effect.

First draft the basic sleeve pattern.

Then draw the vertical slash lines (fig. 1).

In order to maintain the exact shape of the sleeve, don't detach the cut pieces .

For a better shape, divide the sleeve into two pieces along the seam line situated near the underarm line (fig. 1). (Although note that this is not obligatory but depends on the desired shape.)

Spread out the pieces for the top part of the sleeve at regular intervals, keeping the central line of the sleeve vertical (fig. 2). Make sure that the ends of the head of the sleeve are on the horizontal line. Re-draw the pattern.

Do the same for the lower part of the sleeve (fig. 3). Before re-drawing the finished sleeve pattern, make sure that the exterior length of the two parts is identical.

Don't forget to put in several sewing notches, and to add a seam allowance of 1cm (½in.) to each part of the finished pattern.

78

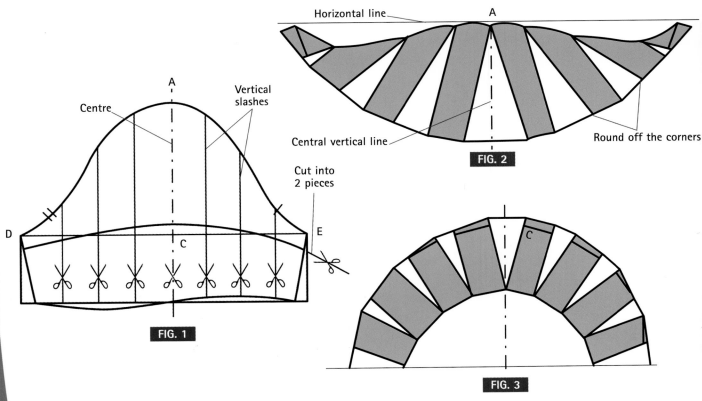

Cap sleeve

This little sleeve needs to fit the bodice armhole without any ease. The finished pattern only has part of the sleeve head, and this is why it is very important that the sleeve is neither too tight nor too loose (in general the ease is 1–2cm/⅜–¾in. when making the basic sleeve).

Lower the sleeve edge by about 2cm (¾in.) at the back (fig. 2).

Mark the position of the sleeve on the armhole with notches to help with assembly (fig. 1).

Make the inner facing for the armhole and for the bottom of the sleeve, unless the whole garment is to be lined fig. 3).

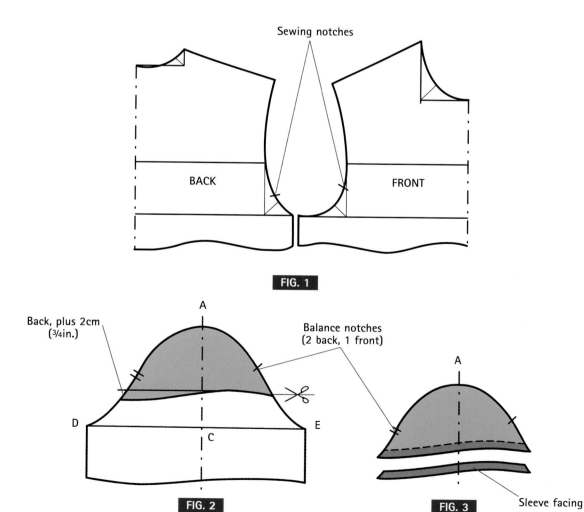

Sewing notches

BACK   FRONT

FIG. 1

Back, plus 2cm (¾in.)

A

Balance notches (2 back, 1 front)

A

D   E

C

FIG. 2

Sleeve facing

FIG. 3

79

SLEEVES

Puff sleeve

If the garment is not made with stiff material, for example, grosgrain or taffeta, use an interior lining, such as a little cushion or shoulder pad, or a canvas stiffening for the head of the sleeve.

Begin by drafting the basic sleeve pattern according to the length and depth of the armhole, giving the sleeve a length of about 20cm (8in.).

Draw the vertical slash lines, as shown in fig. 1, to increase the sleeve width and volume, and horizontal slash lines to increase the height.

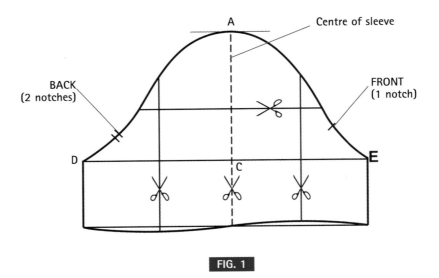

FIG. 1

Spread out the cut pieces at regular intervals, keeping the central line of the sleeve vertical (fig. 2). The more spread out the pieces are, the greater the volume of the sleeve.

Re-draw the sleeve pattern, rounding off the angles formed by spreading out the pieces.

Put in the balance and sewing notches, and add a seam allowance of 1cm (⅜in.) all around the finished pattern pieces.

Make a band at least 3–4 cm (1¼–1½in.) wide with a length equal to the upper arm girth (fig. 4). This band will serve as a cuff into which the volume of the sleeve will be gathered.

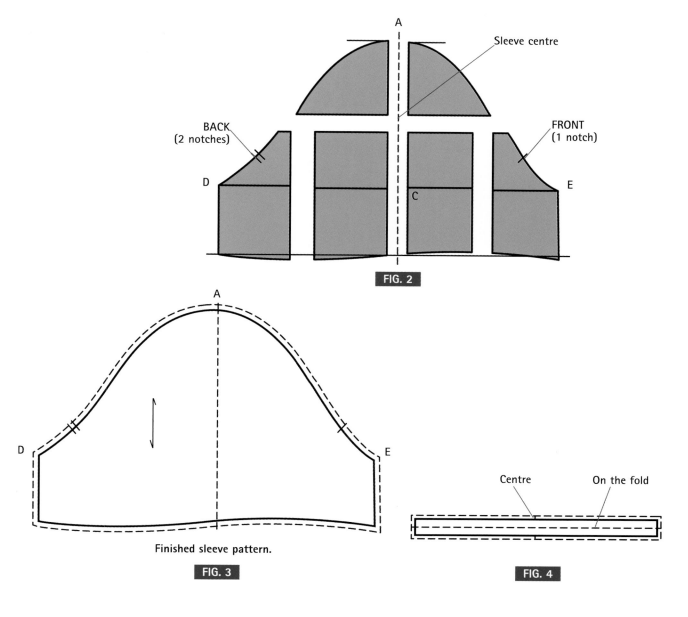

FIG. 2

Finished sleeve pattern.

FIG. 3

FIG. 4

SLEEVES

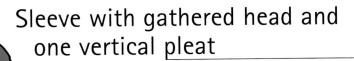

Sleeve with gathered head and one vertical pleat

Style 12

First, draft the basic sleeve pattern according to the length and depth of the armhole.

As this style requires an increase in the volume of the sleeve head, use the 'sunray' slash technique (see p.66) as shown in fig. 1.

Divide the sleeve into two parts down the middle, in order to obtain a dart which will give the effect of a false pleat in the centre of the sleeve (figs 1 and 3).

The bottom of the sleeve will need a facing of 3–4 cm (1¼–1½in.), the same shape as the sleeve (fig. 2). Draw this facing, and trace it out, before cutting.

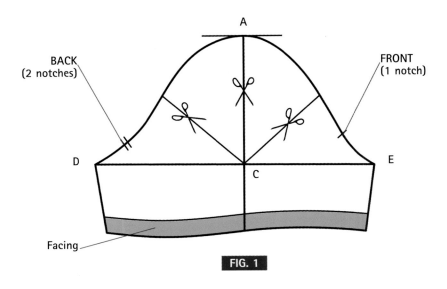

A

BACK
(2 notches)

FRONT
(1 notch)

D

C

E

Facing

FIG. 1

Sleeve facing

FIG. 2

Spread out the cut pieces as shown in fig. 3.

Re-draw the outline of the pattern, rounding off the angles formed by spreading out the cut pieces.

Don't forget to put in the balance and sewing notches, and add a seam allowance of 1cm (⅜in.) to the finished pattern (fig. 4).

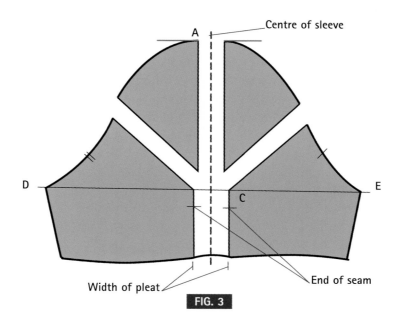

FIG. 3

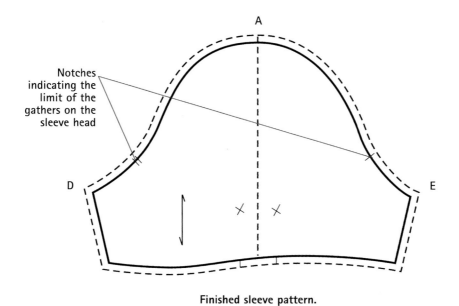

Finished sleeve pattern.

FIG. 4

SLEEVES

Two-part sleeve with gathered head

The sleeve for this style is divided into two parts joined at the centre of the shoulder seam line. Here too, it is essential to increase the volume of the sleeve head.

Start by drafting the basic sleeve according to the length and depth of the armhole. For a more attractive effect, use a fairly stiff fabric, unless the two parts of the sleeve are lined.

Draw the slash lines in a 'sunray' shape, as shown in fig. 1.

Spread out the cut pieces at regular intervals (fig. 2).

Re-draw the outline of the sleeve, rounding all the angles formed when the pieces are spread out.

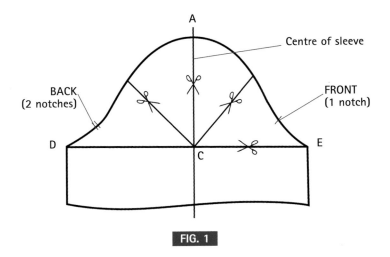

FIG. 1

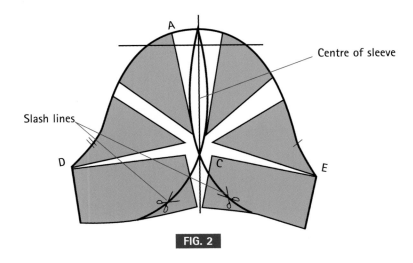

FIG. 2

On this pattern draw the new cutting lines for the centre of the sleeve: these lines are going to define the front and back pieces of the sleeve pattern (fig. 2). Then trace off the two parts separately (fig. 3).

Don't forget to put in the sewing notches and add a seam allowance of 1cm (5/8in.) around each piece of the finished pattern (fig. 4).

If the sleeve is unlined, make a facing at least 5–7cm (2–2¾in.) for each part and trace it off (fig. 5).

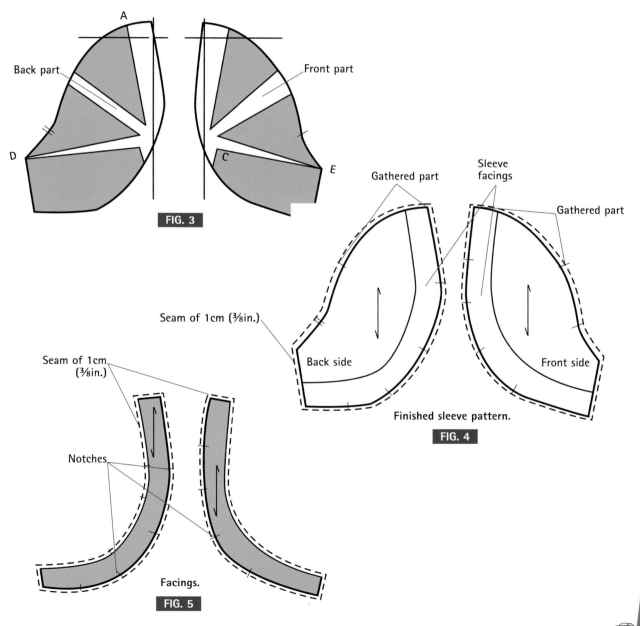

Back part

Front part

FIG. 3

Gathered part

Sleeve facings

Gathered part

Seam of 1cm (⅜in.)

Back side

Front side

Finished sleeve pattern.

FIG. 4

Seam of 1cm (⅜in.)

Notches

Facings.

FIG. 5

Flounced sleeve, Spanish style

In the style shown here, the sleeves have been replaced by 'Spanish style' flounces. The pattern is cut from a circle.

Note that the length of the inside line of the finished pattern (fig. 2) is equal to the length of the bodice armhole (fig. 1).

For two rows of flounces on the same armhole, draw two circles with the same interior line but a different width.

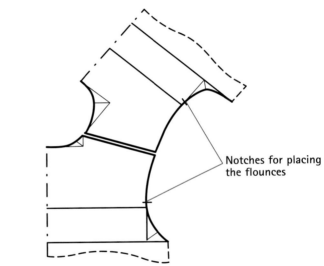

Notches for placing the flounces

Measurement of the length of the armhole.

FIG. 1

For less voluminous flounces, make the pattern furthest from the centre of the circle.

Interior lines for the pattern of the finished sleeve.

For fuller flounces, make the pattern as near as possible to the centre of the circle.

FIG. 2

Wide straps covering the shoulder

Style 15

The sleeve of this style, made in the shape of wide straps, also forms the top part of the bodice.

This construction should start with the back and front bodice patterns (fig. 1), in order to check the length and width of the sleeve.

Lay the back and front bodice patterns shoulder to shoulder (fig. 2) and draw the outline of the sleeve (in blue, fig. 2).

Mark the bottom of the straps on the underarm line.

The line AB on the pattern (fig. 2) is drawn on the bias where the fabric will stretch: hold it in place with a stay tape or, better still, cut the outside edge (the neck edge) on the straight grain (fig. 3), which will put the back and front seams on the bias, and is better for the gathers. Either of these methods can be used: the best choice will depend on the fabric.

Finish by adding a seam allowance of 1cm (⅜in.) all around the pattern (fig. 3).

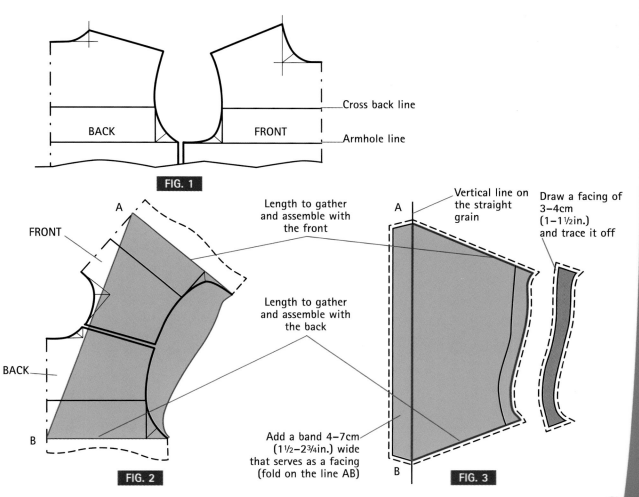

FIG. 1

BACK   FRONT

Cross back line

Armhole line

FIG. 2

A

FRONT

BACK

B

Length to gather and assemble with the front

Length to gather and assemble with the back

Add a band 4–7cm (1½–2¾in.) wide that serves as a facing (fold on the line AB)

FIG. 3

A

B

Vertical line on the straight grain

Draw a facing of 3–4cm (1–1½in.) and trace it off

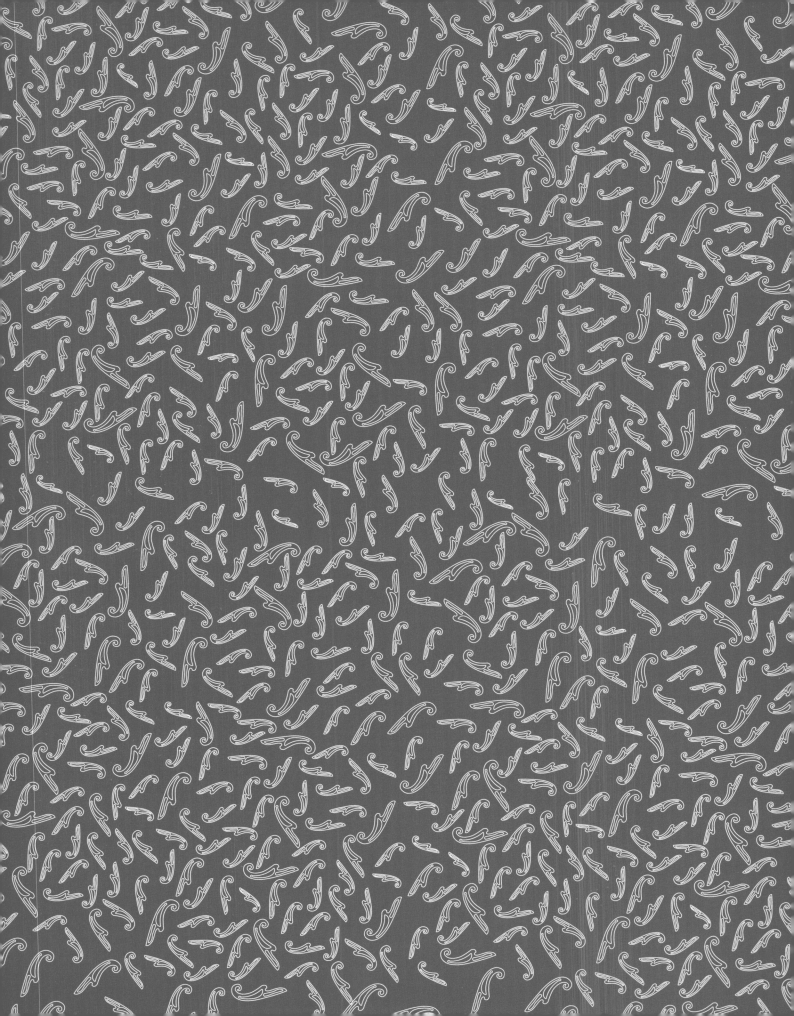

Long sleeves

The styles shown here have been chosen to demonstrate how to master the techniques of drafting sleeve patterns.

Long sleeves, perhaps even more than short sleeves, must be fitted perfectly to the shape of the arm and adjusted at the armhole to allow freedom of movement and enough room for the hand and wrist.

The natural roundness of the arm requires an extra amount of fabric (ease) that must be added to the rounded length of the sleeve head. This amount depends on the kind of garment, and varies according to the shape and style. This is why the basic sleeve block (see p.60) is made without ease.

'Leg of mutton' sleeve

This style is called 'leg of mutton' because of its shape.

To keep the volume of the sleeve in this style, use a fabric that keeps its shape, such as taffeta or grosgrain. If a lighter fabric is used, it will need partial stiffening or some inner structure such as a shoulder pad or a small pad of tulle.

Draft the basic sleeve pattern according to the length and depth of the armhole, then mark the length and width of the sleeve according the given measurements.

As the sleeve narrows at the bottom, add a vertical dart from the bottom of the sleeve to the elbow, to allow ease of movement.

Draw the slash lines as shown in fig. 1. Place the horizontal slash line about 10cm (4in.) below the armhole line (DE) which will give a more attractive shape to the sleeve.

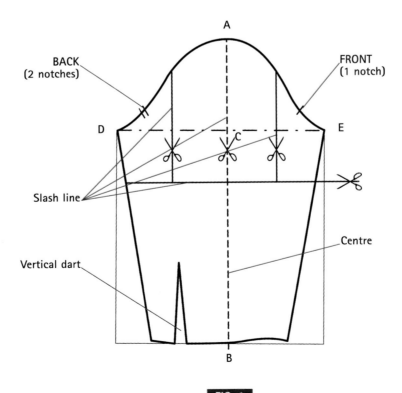

FIG. 1

Spread out the cut pieces at regular intervals in a fan shape without detaching them, keeping the vertical line of the sleeve at the centre (fig. 2).

To keep the shape and proportions of the sleeve head (fig. 2) re-draw the pattern, removing all the angles formed by spreading out the sections.

Put in the balance and sewing notches on the finished pattern.

Add a seam allowance of 1cm (⅜in.) around the sleeve.

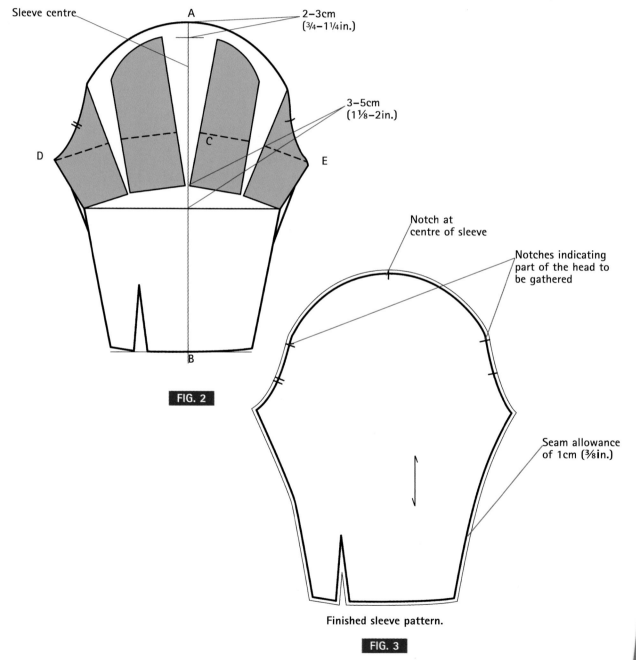

FIG. 2

FIG. 3

Finished sleeve pattern.

SLEEVES

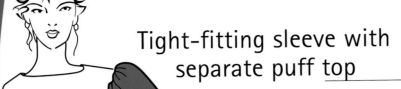

Tight-fitting sleeve with separate puff top

As the top part of this style is relatively voluminous, use a fairly stiff fabric, or interior padding as in the previous style, in order to obtain a good shape.

Draft the basic sleeve pattern according to the length and depth of the armhole, then draw the slash lines as shown in fig. 1.

Put in the horizontal slash line, about 10cm (4in.) below the armhole line (DE), depending on the style required.

As the lower part of the sleeve is very tight-fitting, put in a horizontal dart at elbow level, so as not to impede movement.

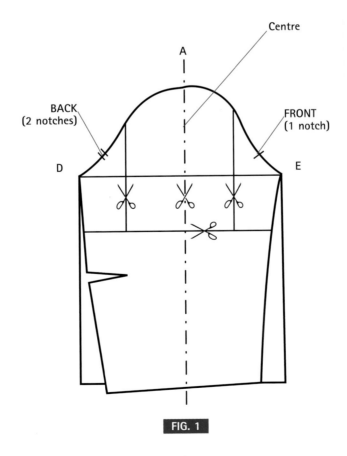

FIG. 1

Cut the top section of the sleeve into several parts (see slash lines, fig. 1).

Separate the top and bottom of the sleeve.

Spread out the cut pieces at regular intervals, keeping the central line vertical (fig. 2).

Spread the pieces horizontally to obtain the required amount of gathers on the sleeve head. If a lot of gathers are required, make more cuts in the top of the sleeve (6, 8 or 10) to help draw the new pattern.

Re-draw the outline of the sleeve, raising the head by 5–7cm (2–2¾in.) and rounding the bottom by 2–3cm (¾–1⅛in.) to obtain the desired gathers and volume.

Add a seam allowance of 1cm (⅜in.) all around the two pieces of the sleeve. Put in the balance and sewing notches on the finished pattern.

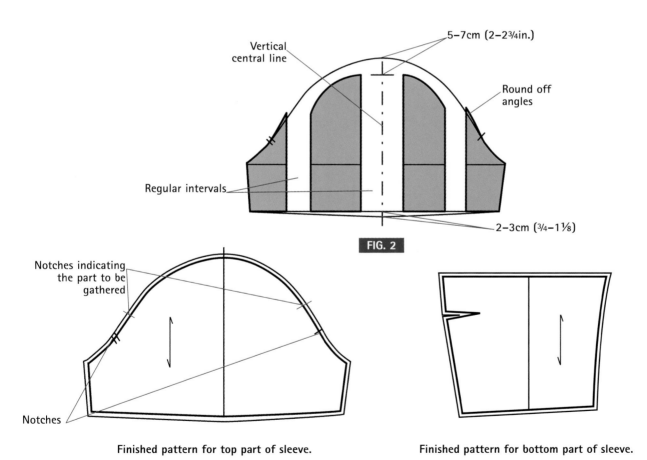

Vertical central line

5–7cm (2–2¾in.)

Round off angles

Regular intervals

2–3cm (¾–1⅛)

FIG. 2

Notches indicating the part to be gathered

Notches

Finished pattern for top part of sleeve.

FIG. 3

Finished pattern for bottom part of sleeve.

FIG. 4

SLEEVES

Sleeve with gathered section

For a good shape, support the gathered part of the sleeve with an interlining, shoulder pad or tulle pad if the fabric is not stiff enough.

Draft the basic sleeve pattern according to the length and depth of the armhole, then draw the slash lines, as shown in fig. 1.

For this style, place the length of the vertical seam line above the elbow. However, it is also perfectly possible to make it longer or shorter.

Because the width and the gathers are above the elbow, make a vertical dart at the wrist, so as not to impede movement.

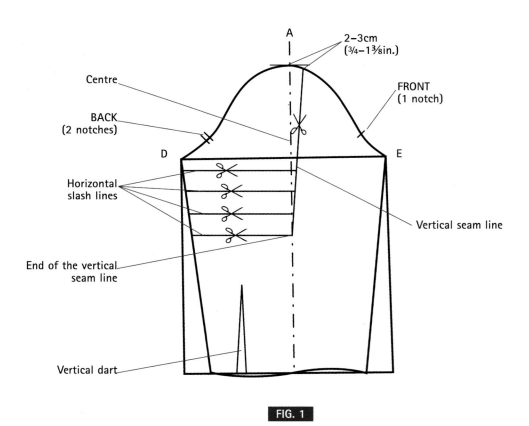

FIG. 1

Spread out the cut pieces at regular intervals, keeping the central line of the sleeve vertical (fig. 2).

Re-draw the pattern, extending the front part of the sleeve up to the vertical line (fig. 2).

Add a seam allowance of 1cm (⅜in.). Finish the gathered part with a seam very gradually tapered up to the central line of the sleeve.

Don't forget to put the balance and sewing notches on the finished pattern.

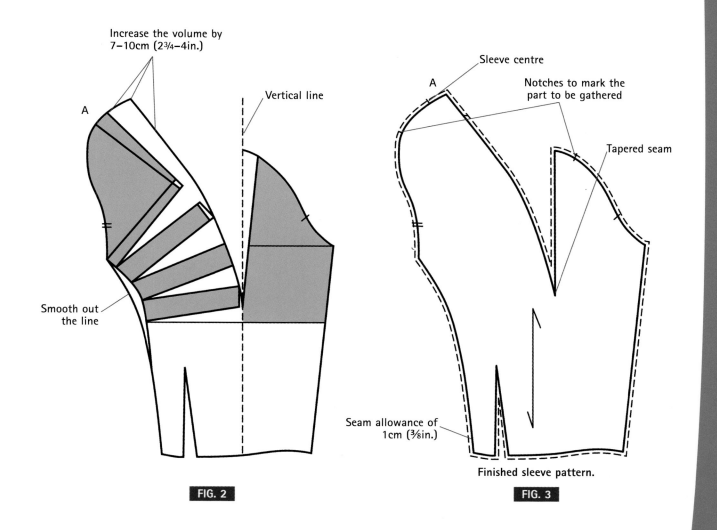

FIG. 2

FIG. 3

Increase the volume by 7–10cm (2¾–4in.)

A

Vertical line

Smooth out the line

Sleeve centre

A

Notches to mark the part to be gathered

Tapered seam

Seam allowance of 1cm (⅜in.)

Finished sleeve pattern.

SLEEVES

Sleeve gathered at the wrist

To give a good shape to the gathered part of the sleeve, use a fairly stiff fabric, or add support to it with interlining.

Draft the basic sleeve pattern according to the length and depth of the armhole, then draw the slash lines as shown in fig. 1. Cut the pieces without detaching them at the sleeve head in order to keep the exact shape of its outline.

Mark where the gathers are to start, ideally in the middle of the sleeve, between the wrist and elbow.

Lower the horizontal seam line by about 2cm (¾in.) at the back of the sleeve for a more attractive effect.

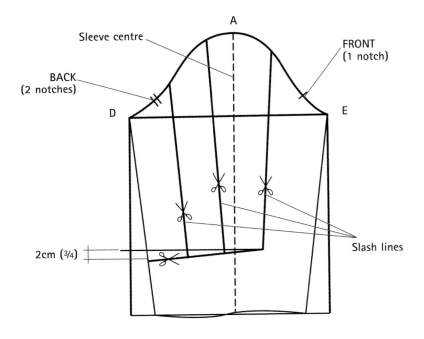

FIG. 1

Spread out the cut pieces, as shown in fig. 2. The more they are spread out, the larger the volume of the sleeve.

Re-draw the pattern. To gain volume on the gathered part, round off and enlarge the bottom by 3–5cm (1⅛–2in.) (fig. 2).

The gathered part is finished off with a tapered seam during making up.

Add a seam allowance of 1cm (½in.) all around the finished sleeve pattern.

Put in the balance notches (centre of sleeve) and sewing notches on the finished pattern. The top and bottom parts of the sleeve must join up again after the gathers have been made to bring the sleeve back into line.

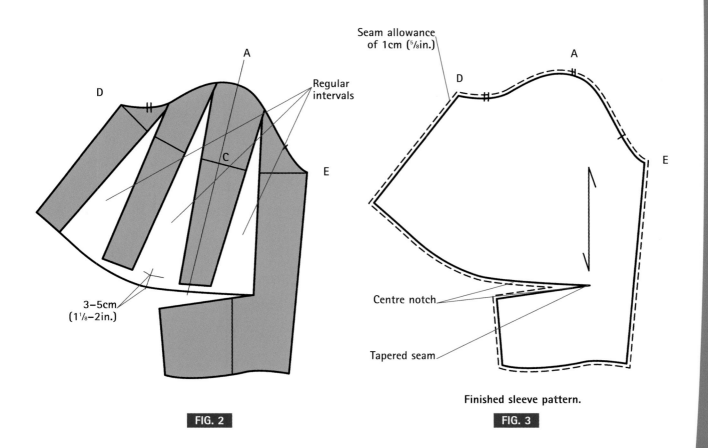

FIG. 2

FIG. 3

Finished sleeve pattern.

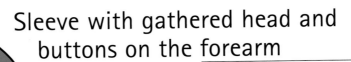

Sleeve with gathered head and buttons on the forearm

Draft the basic sleeve pattern according to the length and depth of the armhole before making the necessary alterations. Support the volume of gathers at the head with a tulle pad or a shoulder pad, or use a stiff fabric.

Draw the slash lines as shown in fig. 1. Place the horizontal slash line on or under the elbow line, which saves having to add a dart.

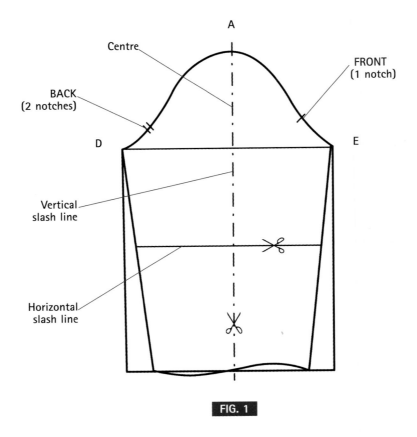

FIG. 1

For this style, place the buttons (edge to edge) on the central line of the sleeve (fig. 1). Alternatively, they can be moved towards the front or back as desired.

Decide the width of the pleat which will be formed when buttoned, about 5cm (2in.) on each side of the central line (fig. 2) is recommended, then spread out the back and front pieces by this amount.

To obtain the volume at the head of the sleeve, raise the two top pieces by 2–3cm (¾–1⅛in.) at the centre of the pattern.

Re-draw the finished sleeve pattern, rounding off the head.

Mark the position of the buttons on the back part of the sleeve, to correspond with the marks for the loops on the front part.

Put in the balance and sewing notches on the finished pattern.

Add a seam allowance of 1cm (⅜in.) all around the sleeve.

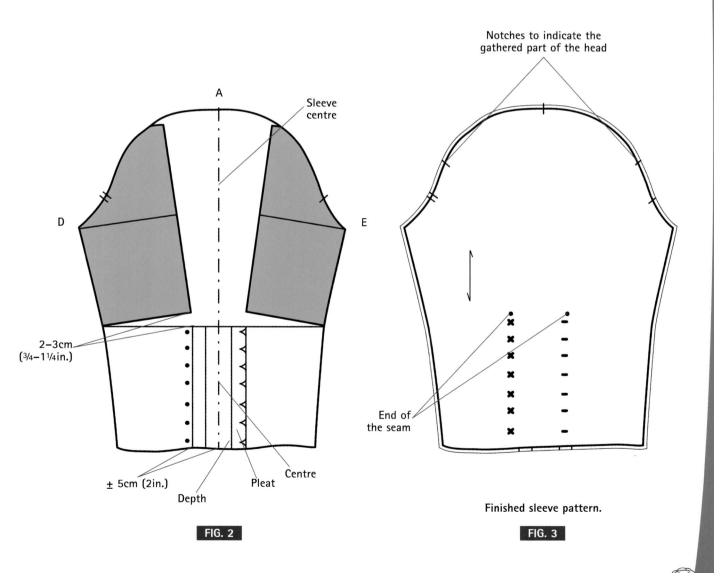

FIG. 2

FIG. 3

Finished sleeve pattern.

Butterfly sleeve (or bell sleeve)

First, draft the basic sleeve pattern according to the length and depth of the armhole.

Mark the length of the sleeve, then draw the slash lines (fig. 1) using the vertical slash technique (see p.63). To draw the pattern for a very wide sleeve, divide the basic pattern into 8, 10, 12 or more pieces. For a less flared sleeve, four to six pieces are enough.

Don't detach the cut pieces in order to keep the exact length of the sleeve head.

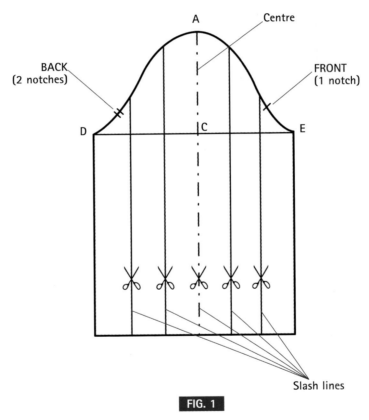

FIG. 1

Keeping the central sleeve line vertical, spread out the cut pieces at regular intervals, like a fan, to the required width (fig. 2).

Re-draw the finished sleeve pattern (fig. 3). At the bottom of the pattern, round off the angles formed by spreading out the cut pieces. Put in the balance and sewing notches and add a seam allowance of 1cm (⅜in.) (fig. 3).

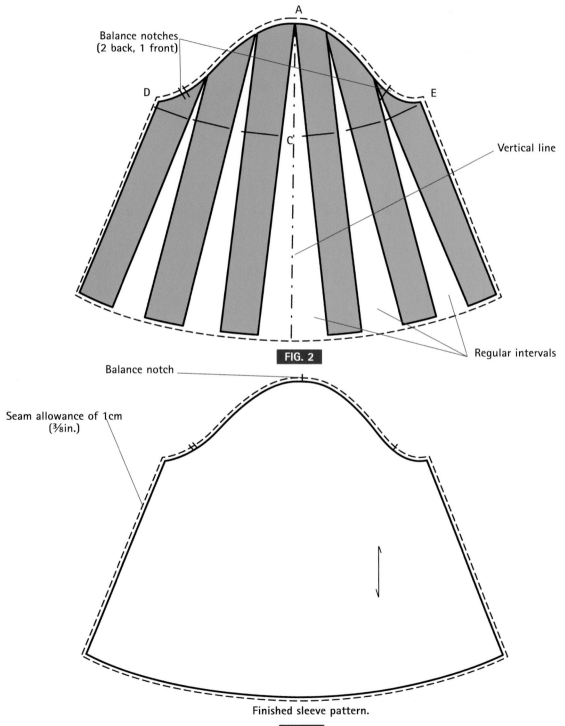

Balance notches
(2 back, 1 front)

A

D

E

C

Vertical line

Regular intervals

FIG. 2

Balance notch

Seam allowance of 1cm
(⅜in.)

Finished sleeve pattern.

FIG. 3

SLEEVES

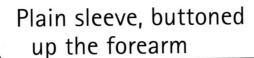

Plain sleeve, buttoned up the forearm

This pattern can be constructed in two ways: with or without a seam in the centre of the sleeve. In both cases you will need a facing at the bottom of the sleeve, either a separate facing, or a hem of 3–4cm (1–1½in.).

First, construct the basic sleeve, with the desired length and depth of armhole (fig. 1).

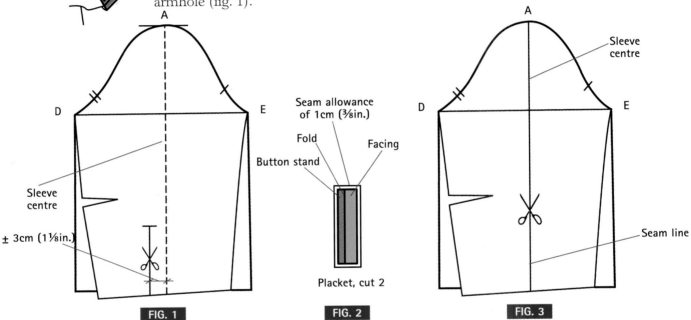

FIG. 1

FIG. 2

Placket, cut 2

FIG. 3

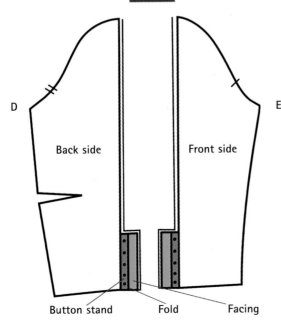

FIG. 4

Sleeve pattern without central seam

Mark the height and position of the opening (about 3cm/1⅛in.) behind the central line of the sleeve).
Make a placket with a button stand 1.5cm (3/8in.) wide, and a facing 3–4cm (1⅛–1½in.) wide (fig. 2).

Sleeve pattern with central seam

Draw the seam line down the sleeve centre (fig. 3). Separate the two pattern pieces: the back and front sides of the sleeve (fig. 4).

On each part of the sleeve add a placket to the desired height, with a button stand 1.5cm (⅝in.) wide and a facing 3–4cm (1⅛–1½in.) wide (fig. 4). Whichever method is used, put in the balance and sewing notches and add a seam allowance of 1cm (⅜in.) around the finished pattern.

PATTERN-DRAFTING FOR FASHION: THE BASICS

Plain sleeve, buttoned all down the arm

Style 8

Construct this style using the basic sleeve pattern, according to the length and depth of the bodice armhole (fig. 1).

Mark the length of the sleeve and the width at the wrist.

Make a horizontal dart at elbow level (this prevents any restriction of arm movement).

Cut out and separate the two parts of the sleeve, front and back (fig. 2). The seam line is the central sleeve line.

To each part add a button stand 1.5–2cm (⅝–¾in.) wide (the width of the stand depends on the diameter of the buttons) and a facing 3cm (1⅛in.) wide (fig. 2).

Mark the position of the buttons on the finished pattern.

Add balance and sewing notches.

Add a seam allowance of 1cm (3/8in.) to both pattern pieces.

Finish the bottom of the sleeve with a separate facing or a hem of 2–3cm (¾–1⅛in.).

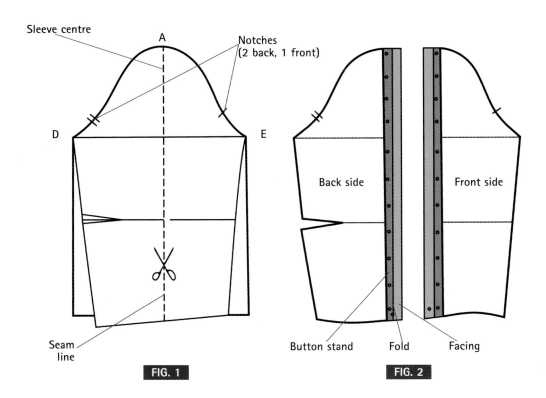

FIG. 1

Sleeve centre · A · Notches (2 back, 1 front) · D · E · Seam line

FIG. 2

Back side · Front side · Button stand · Fold · Facing

103

Plain sleeve with flounces at the wrist
Style 9

Construct this style using the basic sleeve pattern, adjusting it according to the length and depth of the bodice armhole (fig. 1).

Add a horizontal dart at elbow level, to avoid restricting arm movement as this style of sleeve is fairly close-fitting.

Mark the length of the sleeve and the width at the wrist. Shorten the sleeve by the desired depth of the flounces (for example 10cm/ 4 in.). Make sure the length of the flounce corresponds to the wrist circumference.

The volume of flounce depends on the arc drawn between points A and B: the deeper the arc, the fuller the flounce (fig. 2: blue arc, full flounce; black arc, smaller flounce). In this way one can make a flounce of 180° (blue semi-circle in fig. 3) or even a flounce of 360° (whole circle).

Put in the balance and sewing notches. Add a seam allowance of 1cm (⅜in.) to the finished pattern of the sleeve and flounce.

104

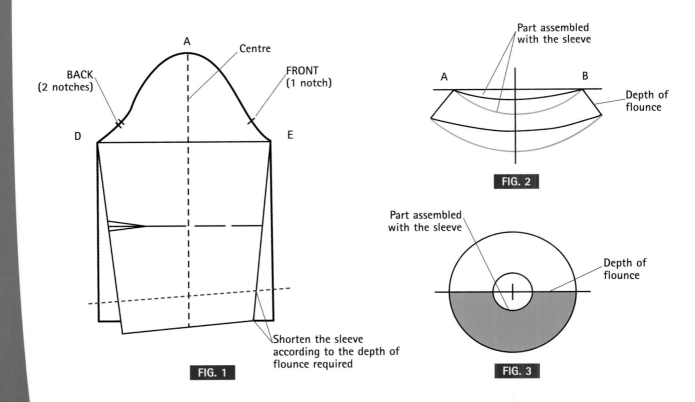

FIG. 1

A

Centre

BACK
(2 notches)

FRONT
(1 notch)

D

E

Shorten the sleeve according to the depth of flounce required

Part assembled with the sleeve

A

B

Depth of flounce

FIG. 2

Part assembled with the sleeve

Depth of flounce

FIG. 3

Plain sleeve with separate cuff

Style 10

First, draft the basic sleeve according to the length and depth of the armhole (fig. 1).

To avoid restricting arm movement, make a dart at elbow level.

Construct this style without an opening at the wrist: to allow the hand through, make the bottom of the sleeve wide enough or use a fabric with some give.

Join the two exterior edges of the cuff, either on the central line or 2–3cm (¾–1⅛in.) towards the front or back of the sleeve (don't forget the balance notch).

Make sure the width of the sleeve bottom and the cuff correspond exactly (fig. 2). Add a seam allowance of 1cm (⅜in.) and don't forget to put in the balance and sewing notches.

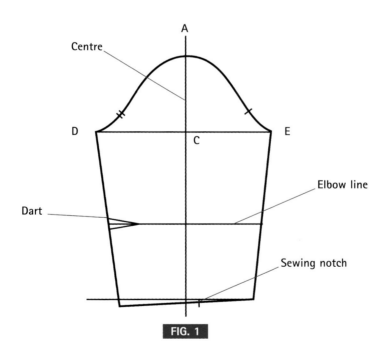

FIG. 1

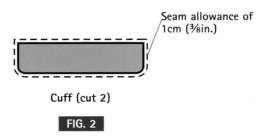

Cuff (cut 2)

FIG. 2

Plain sleeve with shirt cuff

First, draft the basic sleeve pattern according to the length and depth of the armhole (fig. 1).

Put an ease pleat at the wrist to avoid having to make a dart at the elbow. Mark a slit of about 8–10cm (3–4in.) at the wrist (see fig. 1).

Make sure the length of the cuff corresponds to the width at the bottom of the sleeve, after closing the pleat (fig. 2). The depth of the pleat is generally not more than 2–3cm (¾–1⅛in.).

Add a seam allowance of 1cm (⅜in.) and don't forget to add the balance and sewing notches.

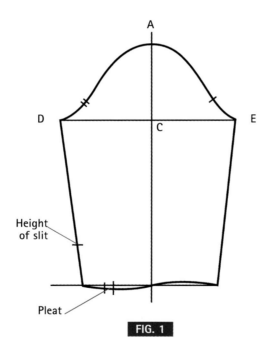

FIG. 1

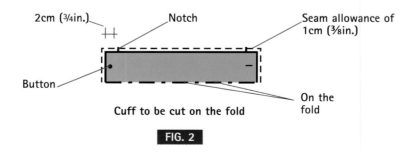

FIG. 2

Plain sleeve with two pleats and turned-back cuff

Style 12

Draft the basic sleeve pattern according to the length and depth of the armhole.

Make two pleats at the wrist in place of a dart at the elbow.

Mark the length of the slit at about 8–12cm (3–4¾in.) (fig. 1).

Make sure the length of the cuff corresponds to the width at the bottom of the sleeve (after closing the pleats).

Place the button to fasten the sleeve near the inside hem of the cuff in order to leave the rest of the cuff free (fig. 2).

Add a seam allowance of 1cm (⅜in.) and don't forget to put in the balance and sewing notches.

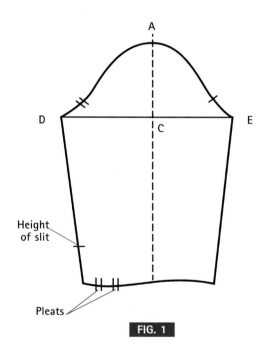

Height of slit

Pleats

FIG. 1

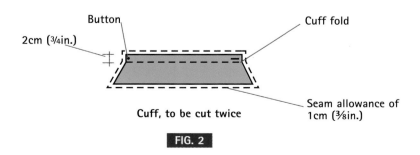

Button

2cm (¾in.)

Cuff fold

Cuff, to be cut twice

Seam allowance of 1cm (⅜in.)

FIG. 2

Plain sleeve with slit at the wrist

Draft the basic sleeve pattern according to the length and depth of the armhole.

As the sleeve is fairly close-fitting, make a dart at the elbow so that movement is not impeded (fig. 1).

Put a slit at the end of the sleeve (to allow the hand through) and a facing. Depending on the fabric used, make the facing by methods 1, 2 or 3.

Method 1 (figs 1 and 2)

Draw the facing with a width of 3–4cm (1⅛–1½in.). It must be at least 2cm (¾in.) longer than the slit.

Trace off the facing.

Add a seam allowance of 1cm (⅜in.) and put in the balance and sewing notches.

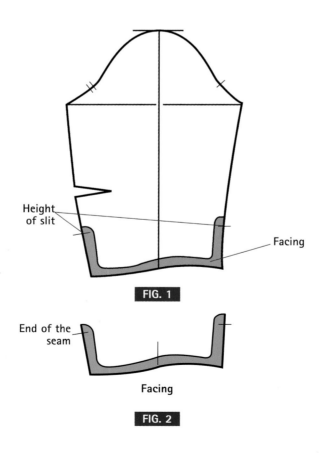

Height of slit

Facing

FIG. 1

End of the seam

Facing

FIG. 2

Method 2 (figs 3, 4 and 5)

The drawback with this method is that it gives four layers of fabric and a seam at each angle at the bottom of the sleeve when the facing is folded in.

Add the facing, with a width of 3–4cm (1⅛–1½in.) and a height of 2cm (¾in.) above the slit.

Add a seam allowance of 1cm (⅜in.) and put in the balance and sewing notches.

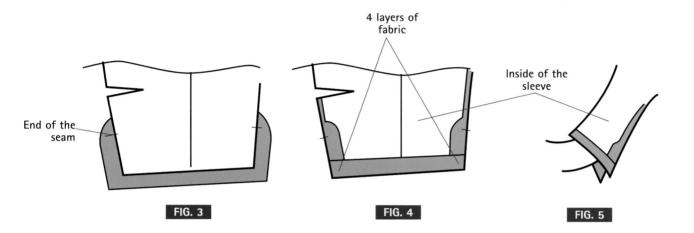

FIG. 3

FIG. 4

FIG. 5

109

Method 3 (figs 6, 7 and 8)

To avoid the layers, cut off the corners of the facing (fig. 6), then make a mitred seam.

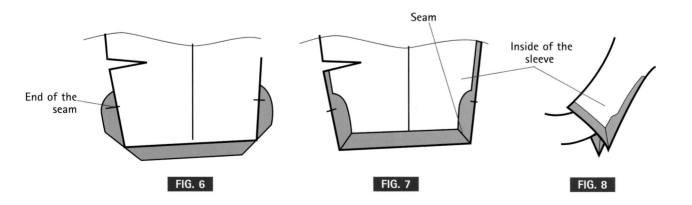

FIG. 6

FIG. 7

FIG. 8

SLEEVES

Skirts

Whatever the current fashion, the skirt remains an essential item in the female wardrobe. From the mini-skirt of the 60s to the maxi of the 80s, whether wide, tight-fitting, flared or on a yoke, the skirt can be made in any fabric without exception.

Two features of the skirt, the waistband and the slit, are studied separately, because of the complex nature of their construction.

For the same reasons as in the preceding chapters, tolerances are not shown on the basic draft. They must be added to the basic pattern when making a particular style, according to the fabric used or individual requirements.

The skirt is independent of the bodice, being held at the waist with a waistband. Waist and hip measurements are adjusted by darts, which is why an opening is needed to put on the skirt, except of course when wide skirts are held at the waist by elastic.

Construction of a basic straight skirt with one dart per half front

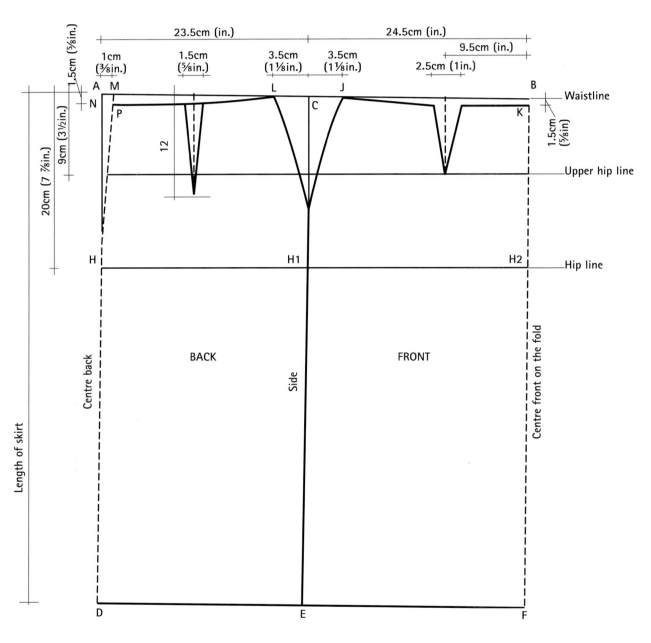

Basic skirt block
(½ back and ½ front)

FIG. 1

Examples of the measurements used in the construction of a basic skirt: waist = 72cm; hip girth = 96cm; waist to hip = 20cm; waist to upper hip = 9cm; length of skirt = 60cm.

1. Draw a horizontal line AB the length of the hip girth divided by 2, in this case 96cm ÷ 2 = 48cm.

2. CB is the half front measurement, or AB plus 1cm divided by 2 (AB plus ⅜in. divided by 2), so in this example the half front is equal to (48cm + 1cm) ÷ 2 = 24.5cm.

3. AC is the half back, or AB minus 1cm divided by 2 (AB minus ⅜in. divided by 2), so here (48cm − 1cm) ÷ 2 = 23.5cm.

4. Draw three vertical lines the length of the skirt (here, 60cm/23½in.): AD (centre back), CE (side line), BF (centre front on the fold).

5. Join D, E and F, then mark H, H1 and H2 so that AH = CH1 = BH2 = 20cm (8in.) (hip level); draw the hip line passing through H, H1 and H2.

6. Calculate the amount of fabric to be suppressed by the darts at the waist. For a pattern of half back and half front: half hip measurement minus half waist, so here, (96cm ÷ 2) − (72cm ÷ 2) = 12cm. Then divide by 2 to find the amount to be suppressed on the half back or the half front: 12cm ÷ 2 = 6cm.

113

This construction technique for a straight skirt with one dart per half front can be used where the difference between the waistline and the hip line is not too great. This basic skirt block can be used when making alterations by 'slashing' (such as for a drop waist skirt, flared skirt or panelled skirt).

Amount of suppression on the half front

1. Half the width of the side dart = CJ = 3.5cm. Draw JH1 with a curved ruler.

2. Place the front dart on the waistline, 9.5cm from the centre front. In general, this amount depends on the cross bust point measurement. For example, if the cross bust measurement = 19cm, then place the front dart at 19cm ÷ 2 = 9.5cm from the centre front; width of front dart = 2.5cm (1in.) at the waistline; length of front dart = 9cm (3½in.).

3. On the centre front line place K 1.5cm (⅝in.) under B and join J with a gentle curve (re-draw this line after closing the dart). Check the amount to be suppressed: 3.5cm + 2.5cm = 6cm.

The number of darts depends on the difference between the waist measurement and the hip measurement: if this difference is very large, put in several darts – two or even three per quarter of the skirt – and divide the total amount to be suppressed by the number of darts.

Amount of suppression on the half back

1. Half width of the side dart = CL = 3.5cm. Draw LH1 with a curved ruler.

2. On the centre back line put in a dart with a half width of 1cm (⅜in.) (AM); length of this dart = as far as the hip line. Draw HM.

3. Put a dart at the centre of ML, width = 1.5cm (⅝in.); length = 12cm (4¾in.).

4. On the centre back line mark point N 1.5cm (⅝in.) below A.

5. Draw PL (where P aligns horizontally with N) with a slightly concave line (re-draw this line after closing the dart). Check the amount to be suppressed: 3.5cm + 1.5cm + 1cm = 6cm.

This construction technique enables you to easily create a precise basic block. From this you can draft a style to fit any measurements and with any alterations required.

The width of the side dart must not exceed 4–5cm (1½–2in.); the width of the back dart must not exceed 3–4cm (1–1½in.); and the width of the front dart must not exceed 2–3cm (¾–1in.).

Construction of a basic straight skirt with two darts per half front

When the difference between the waist measurement and the upper hip girth is very large, two darts per half front of the skirt are needed.

Halve the amount suppressed by the front dart in the preceding pattern, to divide it between the two darts.

For example, if the width of the front dart in the preceding pattern is 2.5cm, then the width of each of the two darts is 2.5cm ÷ 2 = 1.25cm.

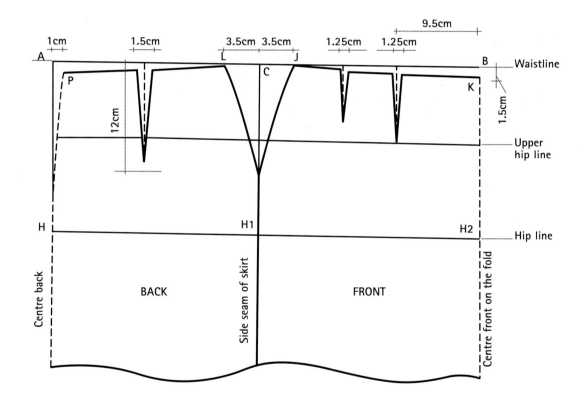

Place the first dart at a distance from B equal to the cross bust point measurement divided by 2 (as in the preceding pattern). Draw the line of this dart and mark its width and its length (9cm/3½in.).

Place the second dart centrally between J and the first dart. Draw the line of the dart and mark its width and its length (1–1.5cm/⅜–½in. shorter than the first).

Fitted skirt

Fitted, figure-hugging skirts are usually made with stretch fabric so that they will be more comfortable. When cutting out, place the pattern on the fabric according to the direction of its elasticity.

To construct this pattern you must know the percentage of stretch in the fabric.

If it is 5% or less do not reduce the measurements and use the basic, classic block. If there is a higher percentage of elastic, reduce the measurements by multiplying them by a figure calculated as below.

Example: percentage of stretch = 12%

Divide the percentage by 2 = 12 ÷ 2 = 6

Multiplier = 100 − 6 = 94% or 0.94

Multiply all the measurements used to draft the skirt pattern by 0.94.

For example, waist = 72cm x 0.94 = 67.68cm; hip girth = 96cm x 0.94 = 90.24cm.

Do not add any tolerance or seam allowance to the finished pattern, as these are included in the calculation.

The elasticity of the fabric means that darts are not needed. Put fusible interlining in the waistband.

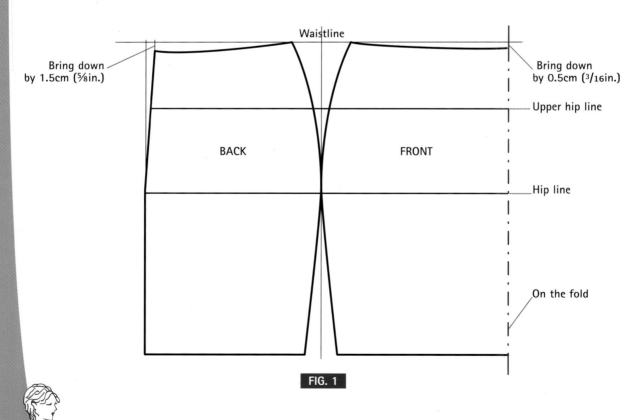

FIG. 1

Waistbands

1. Straight waistband

This is a straight band that holds in the skirt at the waist. Its length is equal to the waist measurement. It has to be comfortable, so:

– it must be folded (to avoid the thickness of a seam); it is often lined with an iron-on interlining to stiffen it.

– its width must not exceed 4–5cm (1½–2in.), otherwise it covers the hollow above the hip bone and risks folding over and spoiling the appearance at the waist.

Put in a seam allowance of 1cm (⅜in.).

Put in the balance and sewing notches on the finished waistband pattern.

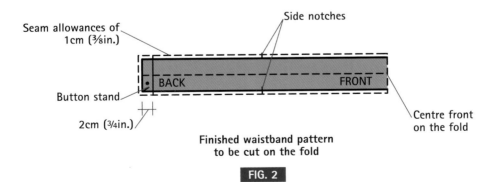

FIG. 1

The amount and position of the button stand depend on the button size and the style of waistband. It is usually added to one end of the waistband.

Seam allowances of 1cm (⅜in.)

Side notches

Button stand

2cm (¾in.)

BACK   FRONT

Centre front on the fold

Finished waistband pattern to be cut on the fold

FIG. 2

Do not add any tolerance to the length of the straight waistband

SKIRTS

2. Fitted, high waistband

This waistband is an extension of the top of the skirt. It is most often used to slim the silhouette.

The facing of the top of the skirt makes the fitted waistband.

Draft the basic skirt pattern.

Trace the line of the waist and copy it parallel to the line of the waist at the desired height. Height above the waist should be about 10–15cm (4–6in.) (if the waistband is higher, it will need to be held up by straps). Depth below the waist should be about 5–10cm (2–4in.) (fig. 1).

To follow the shape of the body, add about 1.5cm (⅝in.) at the sides (fig. 1).

Cut out the waistband on the same pattern and in the same fabric as the skirt, or in lining fabric.

Apply an iron-on/fusible interlining to make it more rigid.

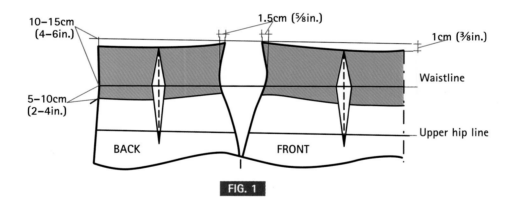

FIG. 1

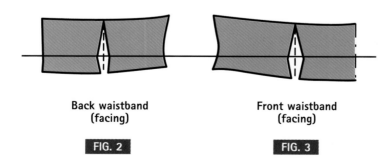

Back waistband
(facing)

Front waistband
(facing)

FIG. 2

FIG. 3

3 Separate waistband for a low waist

To construct this pattern, start by drafting the flared skirt pattern (figs 2 and 3, style 4, p.137).

The best place for the waistband is on the upper hip line, which is about 10cm (4in.) below the waist. The width is usually 3–5cm (1⅛–2in.).

Copy exactly the curve of the waistline and draw it once above the upper hip line, and then again below the upper hip line. The two new lines should be separated by the width of the waistband and must be parallel to the waistline.

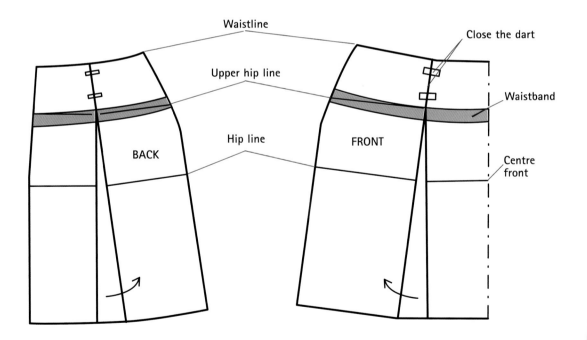

FIG. 1

Then separate the two parts: the waistband and the bottom of flared skirt. Trace off the bottom of the skirt pattern (figs 4 and 5).

Add a seam allowance of 1cm (⅜in.). Put in balance and sewing notches.

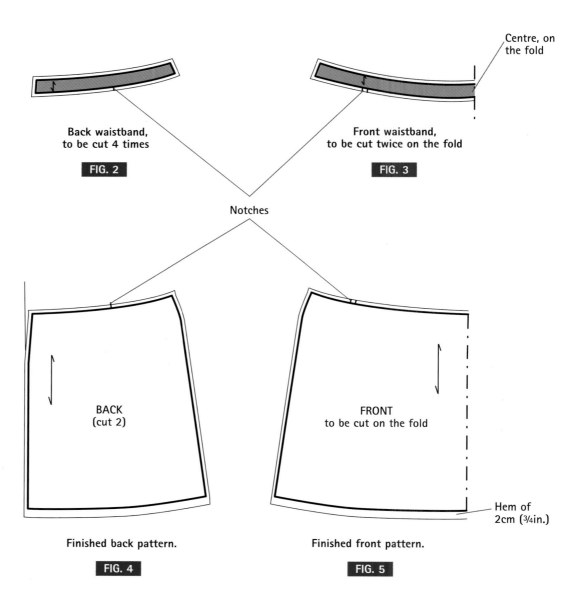

Centre, on the fold

Back waistband,
to be cut 4 times

FIG. 2

Front waistband,
to be cut twice on the fold

FIG. 3

Notches

BACK
(cut 2)

FRONT
to be cut on the fold

Hem of
2cm (¾in.)

Finished back pattern.

FIG. 4

Finished front pattern.

FIG. 5

4. Fitted waistband for a low waist

This fitted waistband serves to hold up the top of the skirt and to keep its shape: it is placed inside the skirt. It can be made from the same fabric as the skirt, or from lining, but it must be inter-lined for more rigidity.

To construct this pattern, first draft the flared skirt pattern (figs 2 and 3, style 4, p.137).

Mark the depth of the waistband (usually on the upper hip line) as shown in fig. 1. Trace the waistline and redraw it parallel at the level of the upper hip line.

Remove the top part of the front and back skirt (in orange on fig. 1).

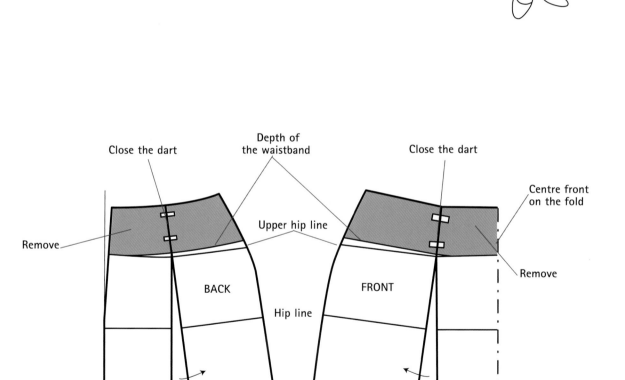

FIG. 1

Then draw the width of the fitted waistband on the new pattern: about 7–10cm (2¾–4in.) (fig. 2).

Trace off the back and front facings (figs 3 and 4).

Add a seam allowance of 1cm (⅜in.). Put in balance and sewing notches.

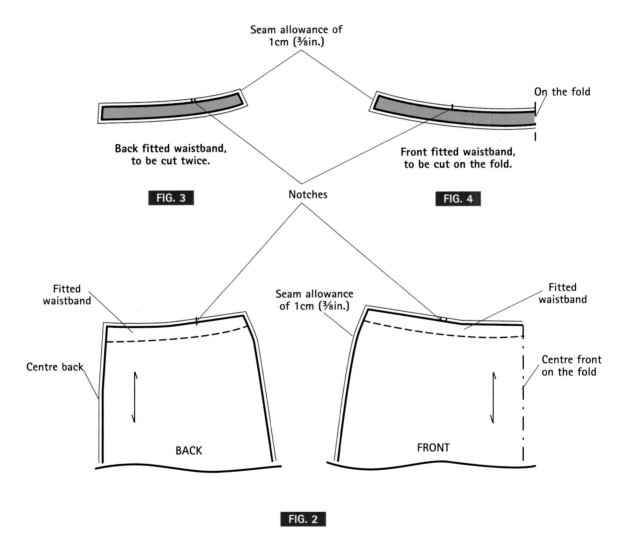

Seam allowance of 1cm (⅜in.)

On the fold

Back fitted waistband, to be cut twice.

Front fitted waistband, to be cut on the fold.

FIG. 3

Notches

FIG. 4

Fitted waistband

Seam allowance of 1cm (⅜in.)

Fitted waistband

Centre back

Centre front on the fold

BACK

FRONT

FIG. 2

122

Slits

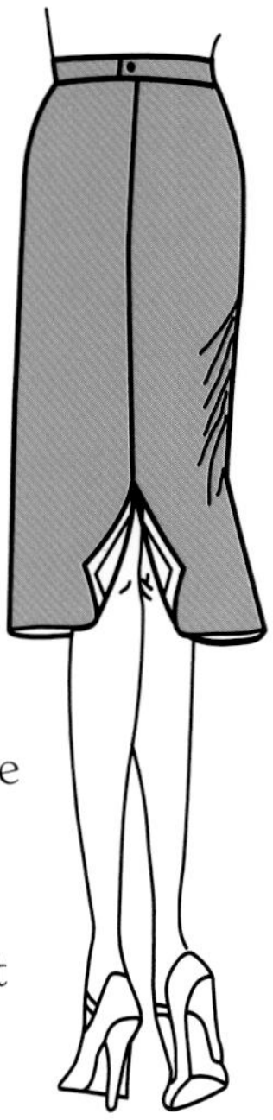

1. Simple slit

In general, slits are made on straight skirts, either to look attractive (fancy slits) or for the sake of comfort, so that movement is not hindered.

Draft the basic skirt block to the given measurements, then mark the height of the slit (here, about 15cm).

The pattern for this style can be constructed in two ways: the choice depends on the thickness of the fabric and the quality of the finish.

First method

This is the simplest and easiest method of construction. Add the pleat amount, about 17cm (6¾in.) long and 3cm (1⅛in.) wide, to the centre back. Also add a hem to the bottom of the skirt, the same depth as the pleat (fig. 1). The disadvantage of this method is that it creates several layers of fabric when it comes to making up (fig. 2).

Second method

To avoid multiple layers, cut an angle at 45° across the bottom of the pleat and the hem (fig. 3). This method is often used in haute couture and the finish is more elegant.

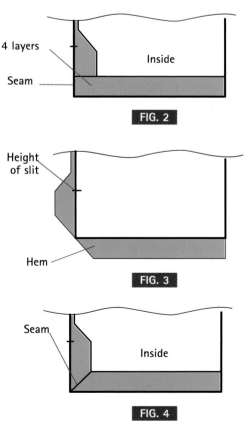

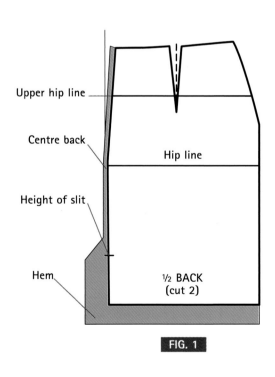

Upper hip line

Centre back

Hip line

Height of slit

Hem

½ BACK (cut 2)

FIG. 1

4 layers

Seam

Inside

FIG. 2

Height of slit

Hem

FIG. 3

Seam

Inside

FIG. 4

2. Slit with a flat pleat, open or closed

In this style, a flat pleat (also known as a knife pleat) is added to the back of the skirt in the central seam.

Use the same pattern whether the pleat is closed or open, the difference will be created at the making up stage: for the closed pleat, sew all along the pleat, but do not do so for the open pleat.

In both cases tack down the width of the pleat, to prevent it distorting out of shape.

First construct the basic skirt block according to the given measurements.

Mark the height of the slit on the centre back (fig. 1).

Add the width of the pleat (3cm/1⅛in. minimum) to the left and right sides.

Put in balance and sewing notches.

Add a seam allowance of 1cm (⅜in.) and a hem that is equal to the width of the pleat to the bottom of the skirt.

The slit with a flat pleat takes on its final shape after ironing: the left side is folded along the centre back line (see fold line in fig. 1), and the right side forms the inner pleat (fig. 2).

124

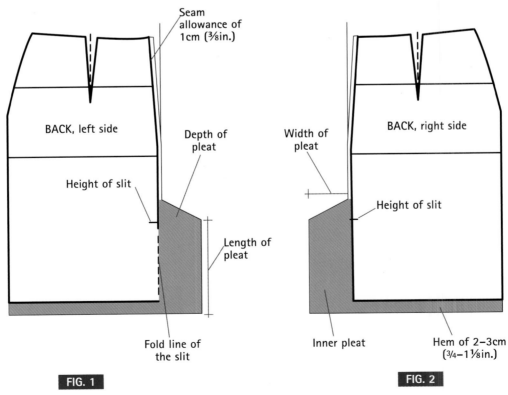

FIG. 1   FIG. 2

3. Slit with an inverted pleat

In this style the pleat is added to the centre back of the skirt. The whole pattern is shown here for the sake of clarity, but it can be constructed on the fold.

Draft the basic skirt pattern according to the given measurements.

At the centre back, mark the height of the pleat then, 2–3cm (¾–1⅛in.) underneath, put a notch to mark the end of the seam (fig. 1).

Then add the depth (fig. 1, in orange) and the inner pleat (in blue), both the same width (usually about 5cm/2in.). If it is made any larger than this the slit can hamper movement.

125

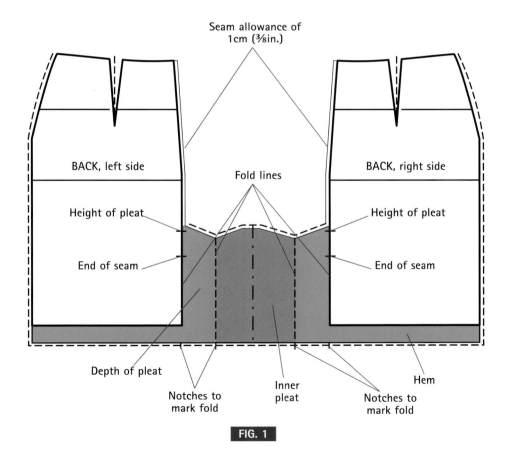

Seam allowance of
1cm (⅜in.)

BACK, left side

Fold lines

BACK, right side

Height of pleat

Height of pleat

End of seam

End of seam

Depth of pleat

Inner
pleat

Hem

Notches to
mark fold

Notches to
mark fold

FIG. 1

SKIRTS

This style can also be constructed all in one piece, but to save fabric it is better to separate the pieces (figs 2, 3 and 4).

Add a seam allowance of 1cm (⅜in.) and put in balance and sewing notches for the pleats.

When pressing a slit with an inverted pleat, make sure that the centre of the inner pleat is in line with the centre back seam of the skirt, which will give a good shape to the pleat.

126

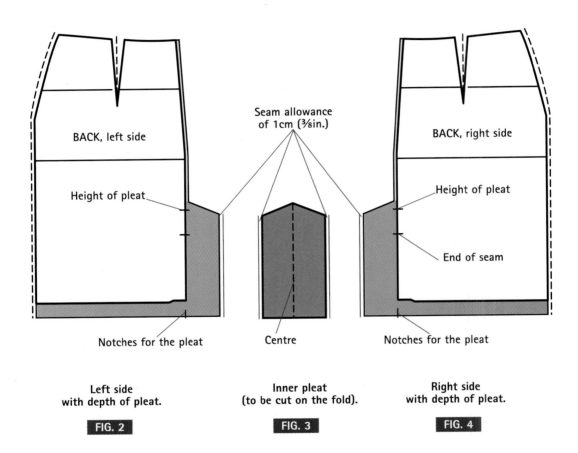

Seam allowance of 1cm (⅜in.)

BACK, left side

BACK, right side

Height of pleat

Height of pleat

End of seam

Notches for the pleat

Centre

Notches for the pleat

Left side with depth of pleat.

FIG. 2

Inner pleat (to be cut on the fold).

FIG. 3

Right side with depth of pleat.

FIG. 4

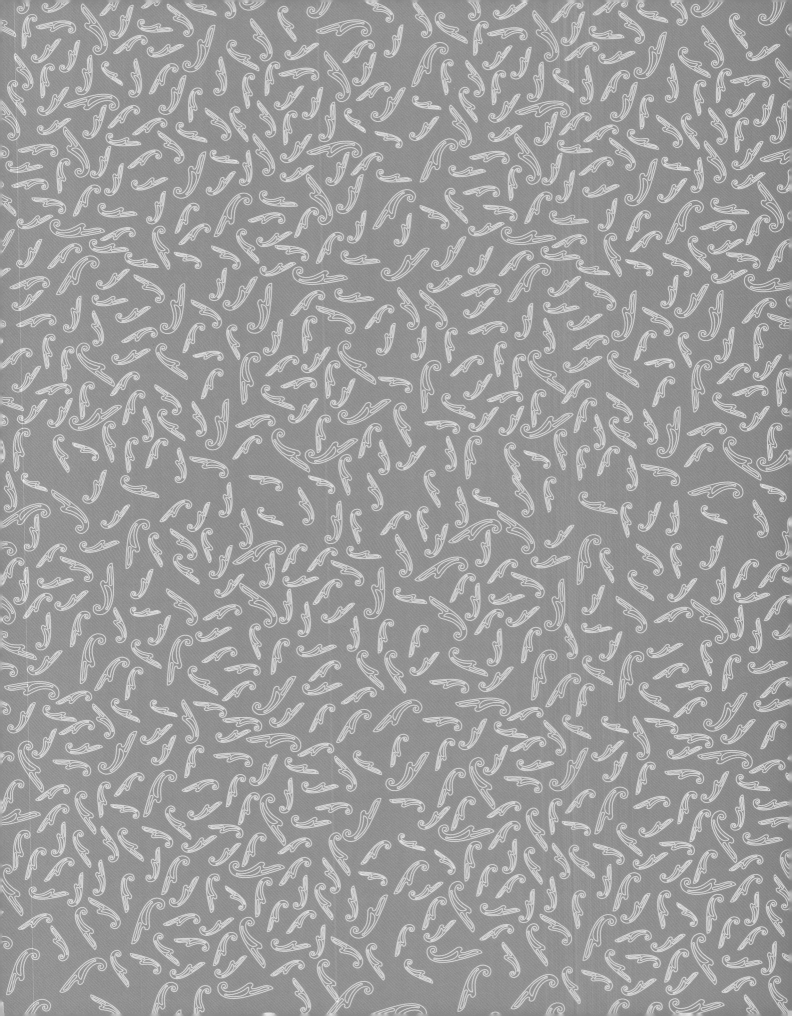

Skirt styles

The skirt styles shown here have been chosen to demonstrate the techniques necessary for constructing skirt patterns (slashing, flaring).

To encourage independence and creativity in the work, some elements have not been automatically included: tolerances, width of pleats or panels, length of slits, placing of fastenings, etc. It is best to decide on these elements before starting to develop the basic block.

Skirt with inverted pleats

To construct the pattern for this style, first draft the basic straight skirt pattern to the given measurements, then apply the technique of vertical slashing.

The method shown here has been chosen for its final pleasing effect, and for the ease of construction.

Extend the lines of the back and front darts (fig. 1).

Make slash lines, then separate the pieces.

Place the cut pieces on another sheet of paper (to allow for drawing the fold lines).

130

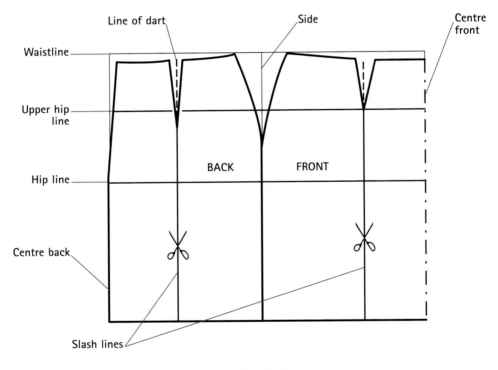

Skirt draft.

FIG. 1

Spread out the pieces to the required distance, as in fig. 2 (here, inner pleat = 15cm). Then redraw the front pattern (fig. 3).

Add a seam allowance of 1cm (⅜in.) to the finished pattern and a hem of 2cm (¾in.) to the bottom of the skirt.

Don't forget to put in balance and sewing notches.

The pleat will be given its final shape by pressing.

Construct the back of the skirt in the same way as the front. Other possible options include: the back without pleats, or with a single pleat in the centre; the back with or without a central seam; or, in the case of no seam, the opening can be placed in one of the back pleats or in the side seam. In any case, the back and front pleats do not need to be placed on the darts lines.

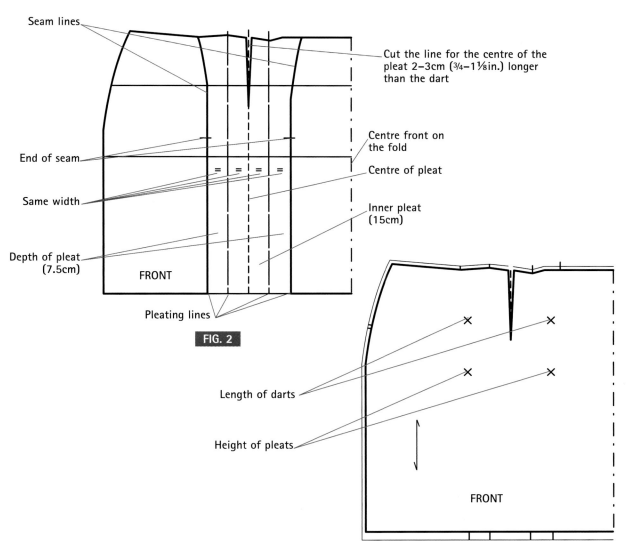

FIG. 2

Finished front pattern to be cut on the fold.

FIG. 3

Skirt with centre back and front inverted pleats

To create the pattern for this style, first draft the basic straight skirt block according to the given measurements, then apply the technique of vertical slashing on the centre back and front lines (figs 1 and 2).

In this style, one can avoid the central back seam that is found on most skirt styles. Place the centre back dart in the pleat, make an opening of 18–20cm (7–8in.) for the fastening and finish with a tapered seam (or else place the fastening in the side seam).

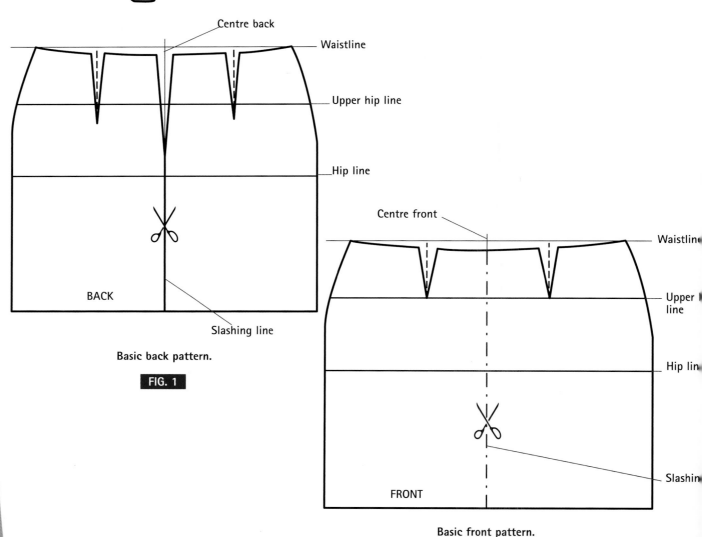

Basic back pattern.

FIG. 1

Basic front pattern.

FIG. 2

132

Separate the slashed pieces.

Place the cut pieces on another sheet of paper then spread out the pieces to the desired distance (here, inner pleat = 15cm/6in.) then re-draw the back and front patterns.

For this style, place the height of the pleat below the hip line (but this is not a rule; in other styles it can be placed at the preferred height).

To make the construction of the pleat easier, make the complete back and front patterns. You need to be experienced to work with half patterns, as problems are often caused by the type of fabric used, most often due to the thickness of the fabric.

Add a seam allowance of 1cm (⅜in.) and a hem of 2cm (¾in.) at the bottom of the skirt.

Don't forget to put in balance and sewing notches.

The pleat will be given its proper shape by pressing.

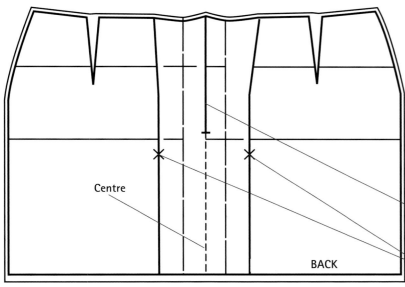

Centre

Opening on the centre back line long enough for a zip fastener

BACK

End of the seam
Height of the pleat

Finished back pattern.

FIG. 3

133

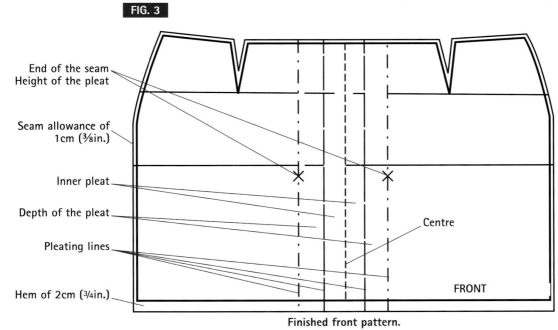

End of the seam
Height of the pleat

Seam allowance of 1cm (⅜in.)

Inner pleat

Depth of the pleat

Pleating lines

Hem of 2cm (¾in.)

Centre

FRONT

Finished front pattern.

FIG. 4

Flared skirt with six panels

Draft the basic straight skirt block according to the given measurements.

As this style has two seams on the front and two on the back, the pattern needs to be made in six separate panels.

For a more attractive effect, adjust the width of the three front panels as shown below.

1. Front

As the front of the skirt has 3 panels, divide the half hip girth by 3. For example: half hip girth = 51cm; 51cm ÷ 3 = 17cm = width of each panel.

As the front pattern is constructed on the fold, the width of half of the centre panel is 17cm ÷ 2 = 8.5cm (fig. 1). If the line of the dart on the basic pattern block is at the edge of this panel, make the seam following the orange cutting lines. If the line of the dart is not on the edge of the panel, move it to the edge.

For the final pattern of the flared skirt, trace off each panel separately.

134

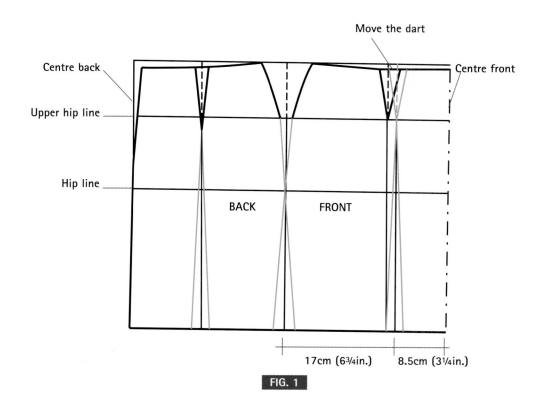

FIG. 1

2. Back

There are two possible options (the first is used here):
– either keep the centre seam and make the seams following the line of the back dart (fig. 1);
– or, in order to avoid a centre seam, proceed as for the front: adjust the width of the three panels and if needed move the dart. In this case, the centre back is constructed on the fold and the fastening is placed on the side of the skirt or in the line between two panels.

Add a seam allowance of 1cm (⅜in.) and put in balance and sewing notches.

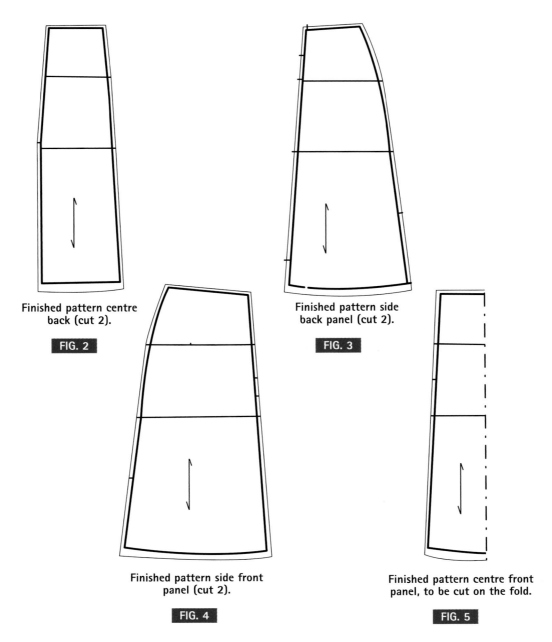

Finished pattern centre back (cut 2).

FIG. 2

Finished pattern side back panel (cut 2).

FIG. 3

Finished pattern side front panel (cut 2).

FIG. 4

Finished pattern centre front panel, to be cut on the fold.

FIG. 5

Flared skirt with no front seam

Style 4

To construct the pattern for this style, first draft the basic block for a straight skirt according to the measurements given, then make the vertical slashes as shown below in fig 1.

Extend the lines of the back and front darts to obtain the slash lines, then separate the pattern pieces.

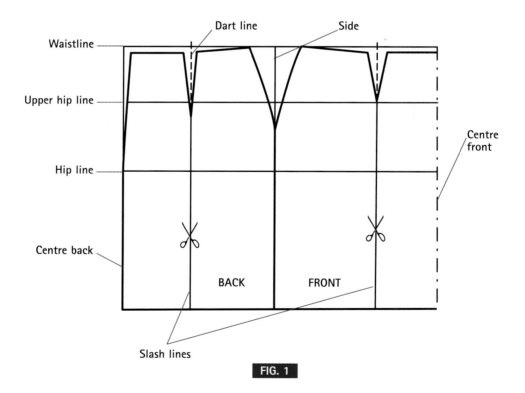

FIG. 1

Place the pattern pieces on another sheet of paper, keeping the centre front and centre back lines vertical (figs 2 and 3), then spread out the side pieces of the skirt by closing the darts.

Re-draw the outline of the pattern, rounding off the angles formed in spreading out the bottom of the skirt.

Add a seam allowance of 1cm (⅜in.) and a hem of 2cm (¾in.) at the bottom of the skirt. Put in balance and sewing notches.

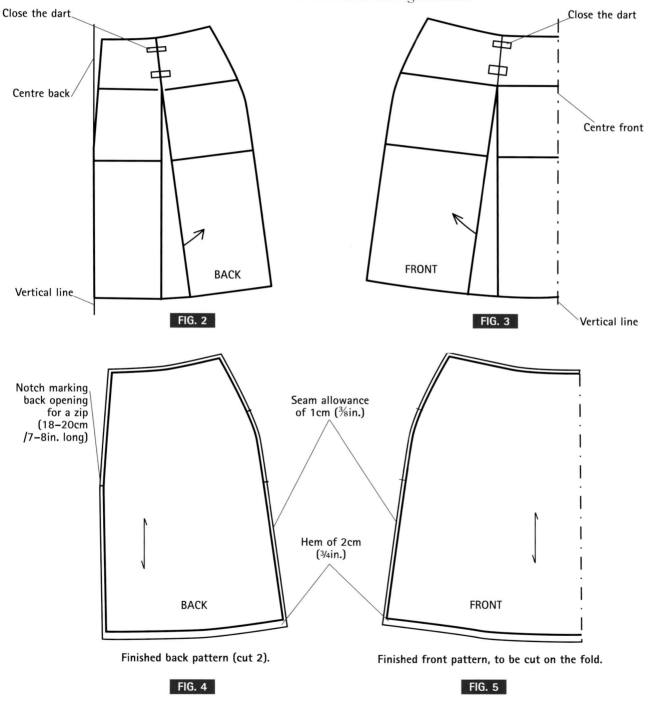

Close the dart

Centre back

Vertical line

BACK

FIG. 2

Close the dart

Centre front

FRONT

Vertical line

FIG. 3

Notch marking back opening for a zip (18–20cm /7–8in. long)

Seam allowance of 1cm (⅜in.)

Hem of 2cm (¾in.)

BACK

FRONT

Finished back pattern (cut 2).

Finished front pattern, to be cut on the fold.

FIG. 4

FIG. 5

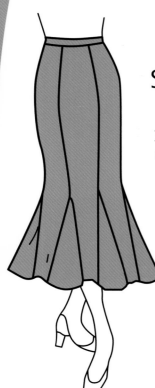

Skirt with godets

First construct the basic straight skirt block according to the measurements given.

Then mark the height of the godets: the best position is above the knee, in order not to hamper movement. In this example, the length of the skirt is 75cm and the height of the godet is 25cm.

Make the vertical seam lines so as to obtain three front panels and three back panels, all the same width (fig. 1). If necessary, move the darts so that they coincide with the seam lines (for how to move darts see p.134, Style 3).

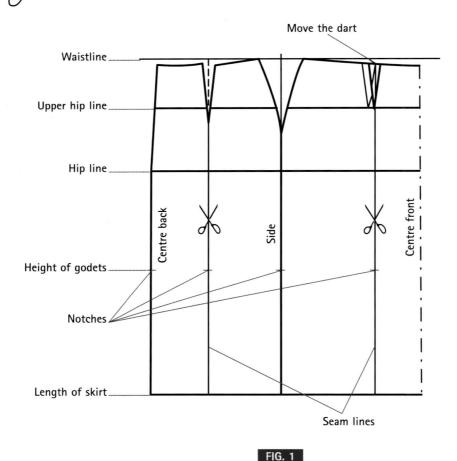

FIG. 1

Trace off the pattern for each panel separately, adding a seam allowance of 1cm (⅜in.) and a hem of 2cm (¾in.) at the bottom of the skirt.

Here, the back pattern is constructed with the seam in the centre. To avoid this, cut the centre back on the fold and place the zip in the left side seam of the skirt.

Construction of the godets

The skirt godet is in the form of a triangle, the length of the side being equal to the height of the godet marked beforehand on the basic pattern. The width of the godet depends on the fabric and the desired style (here, the width is 17cm and the height is 25cm).

Gently round off the bottom of the godet by 1–2cm (⅜–¾in.), to avoid a point on the seam after making up.

When making the skirt, alternate a godet and a panel. For a more attractive effect at the back, do not add a godet in the centre back seam.

Number the panels and put in plenty of balance and sewing notches on the finished pattern as the small pieces all look similar.

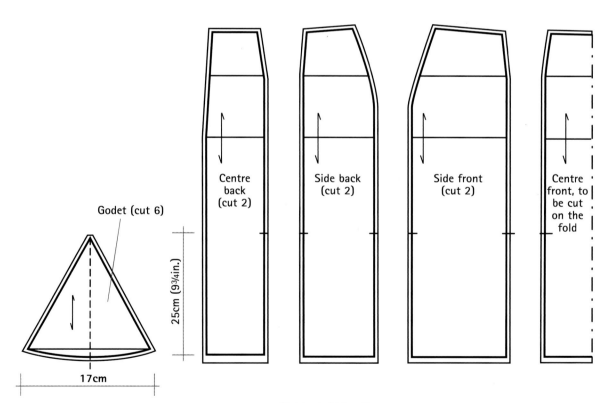

Finished skirt pattern.

FIG. 2

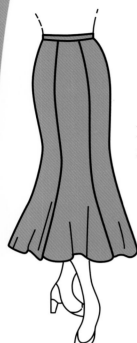

Flared panel skirt

First construct the basic straight skirt block according to the measurements given.

Mark the height of the flare: the best position is on or above the knee, so as not to hamper movement.

Make vertical seam lines so as to obtain three front panels and three back panels, all the same width (fig. 1). If necessary, move the darts so that they coincide with the seam lines (for how to move darts see p.134, Style 3).

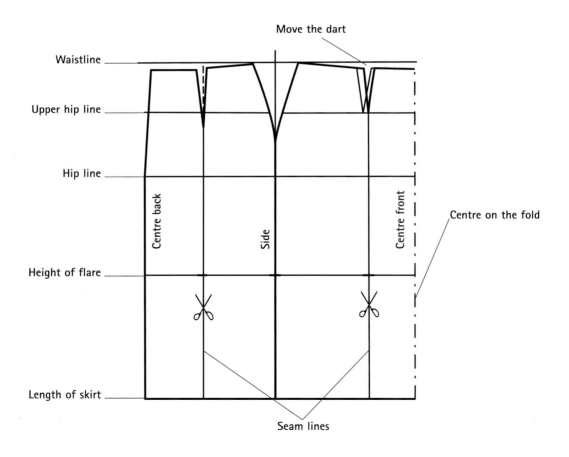

Move the dart

Waistline

Upper hip line

Hip line

Centre back

Side

Centre front

Centre on the fold

Height of flare

Length of skirt

Seam lines

FIG. 1

Trace off the pattern for each panel separately. From notches placed beforehand on the basic pattern, draw the flare lines to the desired width (here, 10cm/4in.). Here, the back pattern is constructed with a centre seam. To avoid this, cut the centre back on the fold and place the zip fastener in the left side seam of the skirt. To adjust the width of the panels proceed in the same way as for the front, moving the dart if necessary. Add a seam allowance of 1cm (⅜in.) and a hem of 2cm (¾in.) at the bottom of the skirt.

Number the panels and put in plenty of balance and sewing notches on the finished pattern as the pieces all look similar.

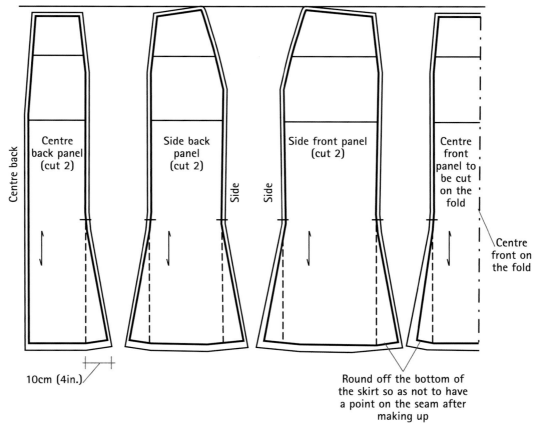

Finished skirt pattern.

FIG. 2

Skirt with a circular flounce

Construct this pattern in two parts, the straight skirt and the flounce.

Draft the basic straight skirt block according to the measurements given. Mark the length of the straight skirt (without flounce). The ideal length is above or on the knee, in order not to hamper movement. Here, the skirt length is 40cm, and the flounce length is 43cm.

The width at the top of the flounce and the bottom of the skirt must be the same when these two pieces, top and bottom, are assembled.

To construct a pattern for the flounce, first draw a quarter-circle at A (fig. 2) with a radius equal to the width of the bottom of the skirt, divided by 3.

Then put a side seam notch measuring half the front width and half the back width of the bottom of the skirt on the curve either side of the side seam position.

142

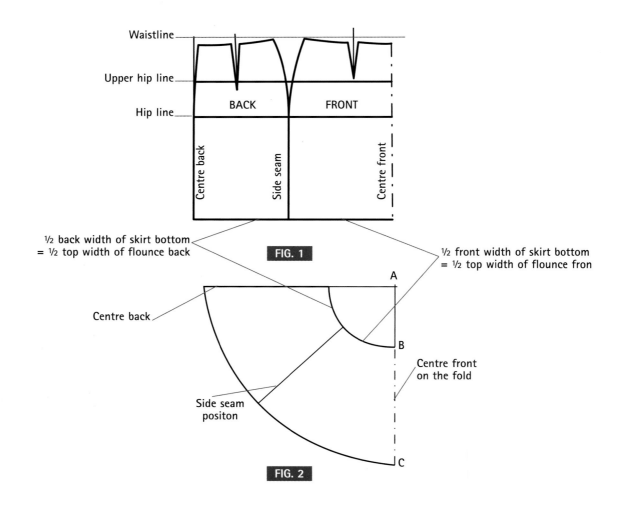

½ back width of skirt bottom
= ½ top width of flounce back

FIG. 1

½ front width of skirt bottom
= ½ top width of flounce fron

FIG. 2

To finish the flounce pattern, mark on the vertical the length of the flounce BC (here, 43cm) and draw the bottom of the flounce with a quarter circle centred on A and passing through C.

The flounce in this pattern is constructed in a half circle, with one seam at the back. For more fullness, make the flounce a complete circle.

To save fabric, make the flounce pattern with seams at the sides and centre back.

Add a seam allowance of 1cm (⅜in.) on the finished patterns of the skirt and flounce.

Put in balance and sewing notches.

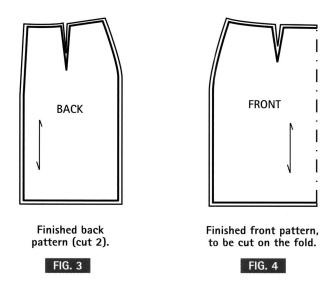

BACK

Finished back pattern (cut 2).

FIG. 3

FRONT

Finished front pattern, to be cut on the fold.

FIG. 4

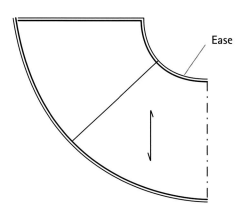

Ease

Finished flounce pattern, to be cut on the fold.

FIG. 5

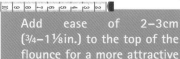

Add ease of 2–3cm (¾–1⅛in.) to the top of the flounce for a more attractive effect.

SKIRTS

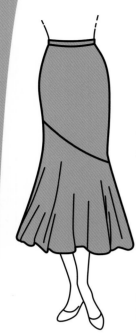

Skirt with bias seam flounce

To obtain the desired fullness at the bottom of the skirt, this construction method uses the slashing technique.

Draft the basic straight skirt block according to the given measurements. Mark the bottom edge of the top part of the skirt with a diagonal line (see fig. 1). In this example the difference in height between the left and right sides is 10cm (4in.).

Separate the top and bottom parts of the skirt.

Round off the bias seam line at each end with a 2cm (¾in.) horizontal section to ensure a smooth seam line and avoid a point at the sides after making up.

144

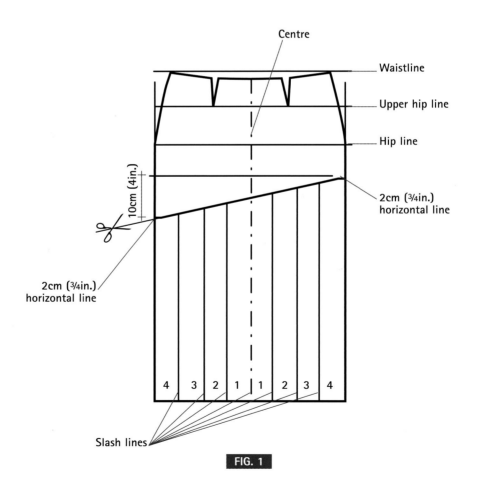

Centre

Waistline

Upper hip line

Hip line

10cm (4in.)

2cm (¾in.) horizontal line

2cm (¾in.) horizontal line

4 3 2 1 | 1 2 3 4

Slash lines

FIG. 1

Divide the bottom of the skirt into several equal parts by drawing vertical slash lines (fig. 1).

Slash up the vertical lines without cutting through at the top, in order to keep the width of the bias line as it is.

Spread out the pieces, keeping the centre line vertical. Start at the centre (piece 1, then piece 2 etc.; fig. 2). The bottom of the flounce will naturally form a circle if the spaces are equal.

Add a seam allowance of 1cm (⅜in.) and put in balance and sewing notches, especially at the centre bottom of the skirt and the centre top of the flounce.

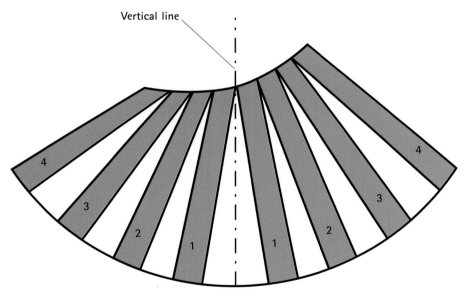

Vertical line

Flounce pattern.

FIG. 2

Circular skirt with handkerchief points
Style 9

Construct this pattern in the form of a square. Draw the two diagonals to the desired length. The diagonal length is twice the skirt length at the sides plus half the waist measurement. The two diagonals form: the two side lines, the centre front line and the centre back line (fig. 1).

At the centre of the diagonals, place the waist measurement in the form of a circle (fig 1). The radius of the circle is half the waistline, divided by three. To balance the skirt, hollow out the circle by 1–2cm (⅜–¾in.) at the centre back and centre front lines (fig. 1 in orange).

As this style is made without any seam, make an opening of 20cm (7⅞in.) for a zip fastener in the centre back line (or the left side line). This will be inserted in a tapered seam.

Add a seam allowance of 1cm (⅜in.) at the bottom of the skirt and around the waist. Put in balance and sewing notches.

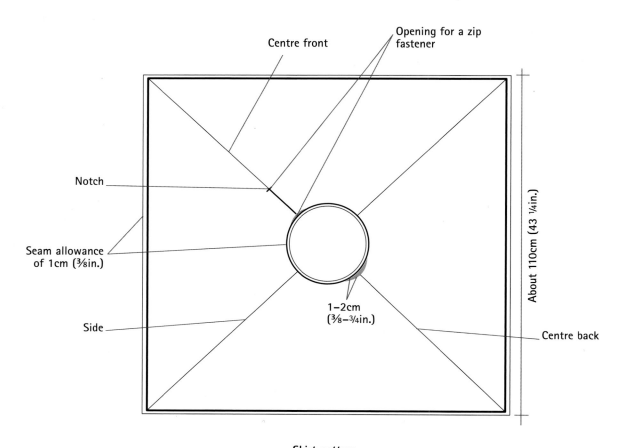

Skirt pattern.

Culottes

Construct the pattern for culottes from the basic block for a straight skirt, according to the measurements given (adding the body rise measurement) as shown in fig. 1.

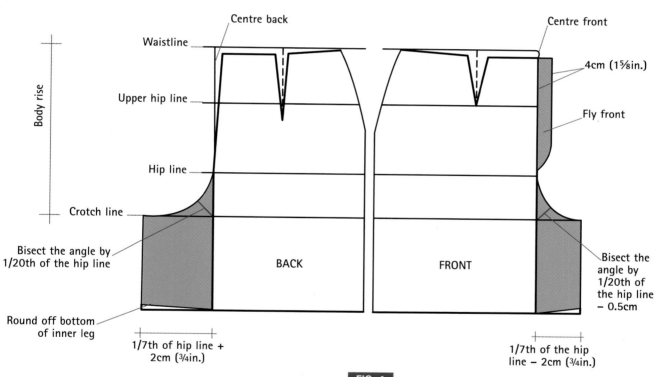

FIG. 1

147

Body rise by trouser waist measurement								
Size	34	36	38	40	42	44	46	48
Body rise (cm)	24.5	25	25.5	26	26.5	27	27.5	28
Body rise (in.)	9⅝	9⅞	10	10¼	10⅜	10⅝	10⅞	11

For culottes, add 3cm (1⅛in.) tolerance to the body rise measurement.

SKIRTS

Collars

A collar can be added to any bodice, whether it has a high or low neckline, and whatever the size.

It adds an important style feature to the front of the garment.

There is a huge variety of collars, all of which need different methods of construction. That is why the styles here are grouped in categories according to the technique used (see p.150). But the basis of construction for all collars, without exception, is the neckline.

Types of collars

Although there exists a great variety of collars of different sizes, shapes, edgings and so on, they can be grouped into two categories according to the technique used to achieve the finished pattern:

1. Applied collars sewn on to the neckline (figs 1 and 2).

2. 'Grown-on' collars cut in one with the garment, forming an extension of the bodice up to the neck (figs 3 and 4).

The first category, applied collars, can also be subdivided according to the construction technique:

i. collars where construction is based on the measurement of the bodice neckline (fig. 1)

ii. collars where construction is made directly onto the bodice neckline after sewing up the shoulder. Collars with this shape are often called flat collars (fig. 2).

The second category, 'grown-on' collars can also be subdivided according to the shape of the collar:

i. stand collars which can be low or high, close-fitting or standing away around the neck (fig. 3).

ii. collars that fold back on themselves, close to the neck or on the shoulders, always forming a 'V' neckline (fig. 4).

**Example of an applied collar:
shirt collar (with or without stand).**

FIG. 1

Example of a stand collar.

FIG. 3

**Example of an applied collar:
flat Peter Pan collar.**

FIG. 2

Example of a shawl collar.

FIG. 4

Construction of applied collars, fastened or open-neck

Applied collars can be closed (fig. 1) or open (fig. 2) but the construction methods are similar.

Draw a horizontal line the length of half the neckline (fig. 3).

Draw a first perpendicular line, the centre back line. Mark on the half length of the back neckline and draw a second perpendicular line, the shoulder line. Mark on half the length of the front neckline and draw the third perpendicular, the centre front line.

FIG. 1   FIG. 2

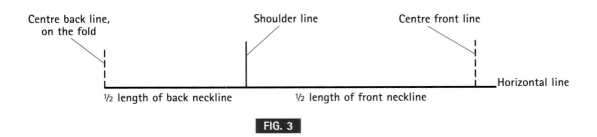

Centre back line,   Shoulder line   Centre front line
on the fold

                                                              Horizontal line

½ length of back neckline   ½ length of front neckline

FIG. 3

Construction of a fastened collar

Drop the half front length by 2.5cm (1in.) below the horizontal line, then divide it into two parts and curve each of these parts by 2mm (fig. 4).

Bring up the back line by 0.5cm (³⁄₁₆in.) and draw a slight curve. This curve gives flexibility as the line is no longer on the grain, allowing the collar to fit perfectly to the neck. If the collar was a straight line, it would pull and flatten the curve of the neckline (especially with stiff fabric) and spoil it.

The rest of the collar construction depends on the desired style.

On the base (fig. 4), add the height of the collar stand (about 2–3cm/ ¾–1⅜in.) and the height of the fall (about 5–7cm/2–2¾in.).

For the back of the collar, the bottom, the top and the fold line must be parallel. Draw the front according to the desired style, for example one of the coloured lines in fig. 5.

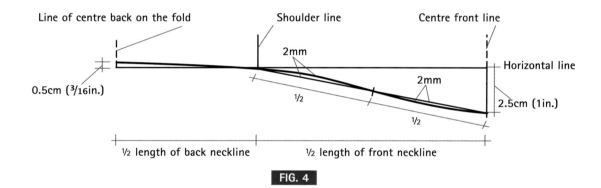

FIG. 4

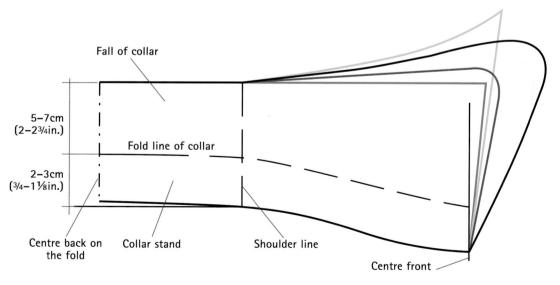

Construction of basic pattern for a fastened collar.

FIG. 5

Construction of an open collar

Raise the front half length by 2.5cm (1in.), then divide it in half and curve at the centre by 2mm (fig. 6).

Raise the back line by 0.5cm (³⁄₁₆in.) and draw a slight curve.

Add the height of the collar stand (2–3cm/¾–1⅛in.) and the height of the fall (5–7cm/2–2¾in.), then draw the shape of the collar, horizontal at the back and according to the desired style for the front (examples shown by coloured lines in fig. 7).

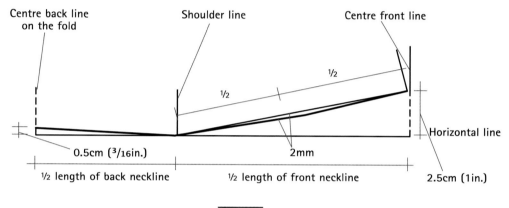

FIG. 6

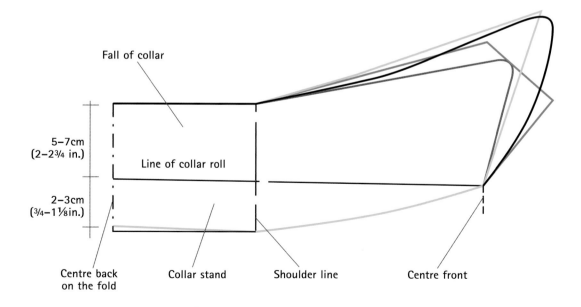

Construction of basic pattern for an open collar.

FIG. 7

Construction of an applied collar with separate stand

The difference between the simple collar and one with a separate stand lies in the aesthetic appearance and in the construction technique. The simple collar is often used for styles in knitwear or loose fabrics. The collar with a separate stand enables you to raise the fall as desired. Men's shirtmakers use this style exclusively in order to give room for the tie.

Simple collar.

FIG. 1

Collar with separate stand.

FIG. 2

154

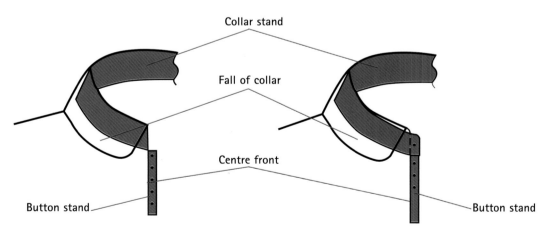

Collar stand

Fall of collar

Centre front

Button stand

Button stand

Simple collar: in general this is applied starting from the centre front and a button stand is then added on the bodice.

FIG. 3

Collar with separate stand: this includes the width of the button stand.

FIG. 4

Draw the desired collar point shape on the collar pattern piece at the outer edge of the base (the centre front point). Give the collar a fall of 5–7cm (2–2¾in., excluding the stand.

Extend the vertical lines of the centre back, shoulder line, and centre front.

Add the width of the button stand to half the length of the front neckline (generally 2cm/¾in., depending on the diameter of the buttons).

For the back of the collar stand, hollow the bottom by 0.5cm (³⁄₁₆in.) and draw the top horizontally 3cm (1⅛in.) away.

For the front of the collar stand, draw two parallel lines 3cm (1⅛in.) apart, as shown in fig. 5. Round off the top of the button stand.

Finish the construction by putting in notches at the top and bottom of the stand: centre back, shoulder, centre front.

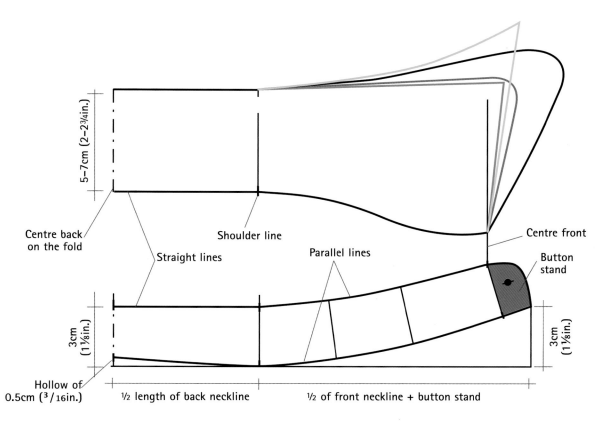

FIG. 5

An exception: the jabot

The jabot is a decorative collar added at the front. It can be made with pleats or flounces fastened at the neck, or based on a circle.

The three styles most commonly used on a blouse are shown here.

First style
Draw a circle with a circumference equal to the desired length of the jabot on the centre front (e.g. length = about 30cm).
Mark the width of the jabot (e.g. about 7cm) and draw a second circle outside the first (which corresponds to the outer edge of the frill).
Draw the shape of the neckline and round off the bottom of the jabot for a good effect.

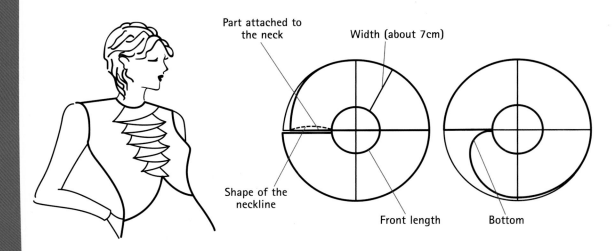

Part attached to the neck

Width (about 7cm)

Shape of the neckline

Front length

Bottom

Jabot in one piece centred on the centre front.

FIG. 1

Second style

Draw two circles for the ruffle (fig. 2A), the first circle with a circumference equal to the neck measurement, and the second about 7cm (2¾in.) away.

Then draw the two circles for the jabot (fig. 2B), the first circle with a circumference equal to the length of the jabot on the centre front, and the second after having marked the width of the jabot (about 7cm (2¾in.). Round off the ends of the jabot.

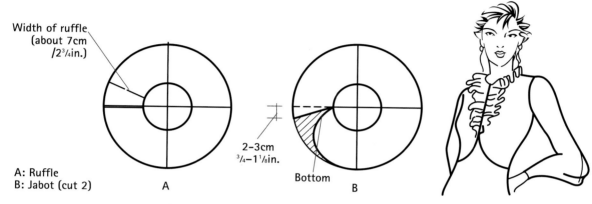

Width of ruffle (about 7cm /2¾in.)

A: Ruffle
B: Jabot (cut 2)

A

2–3cm
¾–1⅛in.

Bottom

B

Jabot in two pieces, with flat collar.

FIG. 2

Third style

Draw a first circle with a circumference equal to the desired length of the jabot on the centre front (e.g. length = about 30cm).

Mark the width of the jabot (e.g. about 7cm) and draft a second circle (which corresponds to the exterior line of the jabot).

Extend the horizontal line and mark the height and length of the collar (the length of the collar is equal to the length of the neckline once the pleats are positioned).

Put in balance and sewing notches.

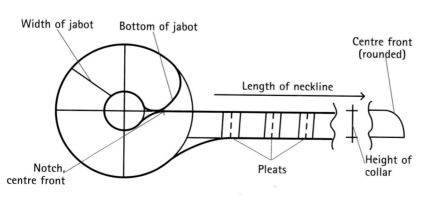

Width of jabot   Bottom of jabot

Centre front (rounded)

Length of neckline

Notch, centre front

Pleats

Height of collar

One-piece jabot extended by a pleated, stand-up collar.

FIG. 3

COLLARS

Applied collars

When collar patterns are drafted separately from the rest of the bodice they are called applied collars: they are applied to the neckline and attached to the garment with a seam.

Strictly speaking the construction of applied collars should always be based on the measurement of the neckline taken from the finished back and front bodice pattern, whether the neckline is round or low-cut (styles 1–5).

Stand-up collars (also called mandarin collars, styles 6–8) are collar stands made by adjusting the height and slope of the neckline. This elegant finish to the neckline can be applied to all kinds of garments.

Flat collars (styles 9–12) are so called because they lie flat on the shoulders. This kind of collar is an exact copy of the shape at the back and front of the neckline. The classic shape, in two pieces with rounded ends placed centre front and centre back, is often called a Peter Pan collar.

Fastened collar with diamond-shaped cut out

Style 1

Begin by constructing the basic bodice draft to the given measurements, then make any alterations.

Draw the cut out to the desired shape and mark the position of the collar (fig. 1, in green).

Draw the back and front facings with a width of 5–7cm (2–2¾in.).

Construct a fastened collar of the desired width using the neck measurements taken from the finished bodice draft (fig. 2): half length of back neckline plus half length of front neckline up to the sewing notch on the collar.

Then follow the markings on fig. 2.

Add a seam allowance of 1cm (⅜in.).

Put in balance and sewing notches on the finished pattern.

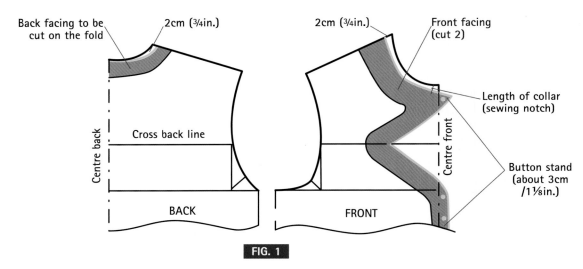

FIG. 1

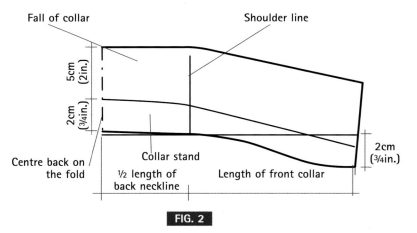

FIG. 2

Open collar
with a V-neckline

Style 2

Construct the basic bodice draft to the given measurements, then make the alterations.

Mark the depth of the neckline (fig. 1, in green) and place a sewing notch to mark the length of the collar.

Then construct an open collar to the desired width, according to the measurements on the finished bodice pattern: length of back neckline + length of décolleté up to the notch marking the end of the collar.

Then follow the markings on fig. 2.

Finish the construction by putting in balance and sewing notches. Add a seam allowance of 1cm (⅜in.).

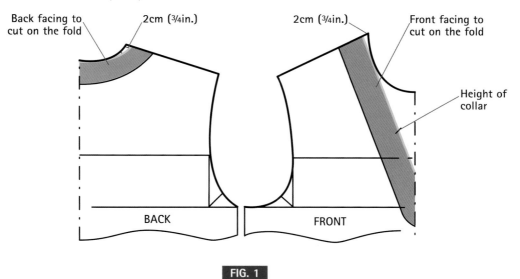

Back facing to cut on the fold

2cm (¾in.)

2cm (¾in.)

Front facing to cut on the fold

Height of collar

BACK

FRONT

FIG. 1

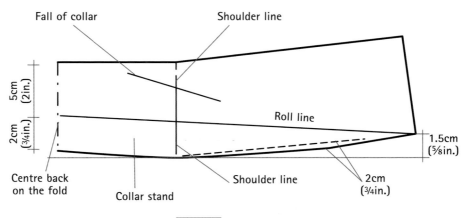

Fall of collar

Shoulder line

5cm (2in.)

2cm (¾in.)

Roll line

1.5cm (⅝in.)

Centre back on the fold

Collar stand

Shoulder line

2cm (¾in.)

FIG. 2

161

Open frilled
V-neck collar

In this style the centre front is fastened with a zip. The frilled collar continues for a few centimetres (here 5–10cm/2–4in.) below the point of the décolleté.

Construct the basic bodice draft according to the measurements given, then make the alterations.

On the centre front line mark the height of the zip and draw the line of the décolleté up to the shoulder line (fig. 1, in green). Then, on the same line, put in the notch marking the length of the collar (collar sewing notch).

Start the construction of the collar by drawing a horizontal line. Mark on it the measurements of the half length of the back neckline, the collar length and the length of the décolleté, all taken from the finished bodice draft.

Then follow the markings on fig. 2.

Put in balance and sewing notches on the finished pattern and add a seam allowance of 1cm (⅜in.).

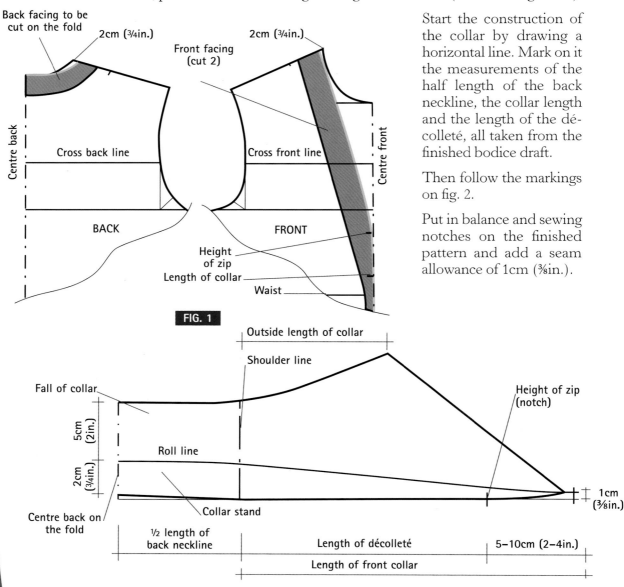

FIG. 1

FIG. 2

162

Open collar with V-shaped décolleté and front buttoning

Construct the basic bodice pattern according to the given measurements, then make the alterations.

Draw the button stand with a width of 2–3cm (¾–1¼in.) (this measurement depends of the diameter of the buttons used). Mark the depth of the décolleté and draw the line up to the shoulder line (fig. 1, in green).

Construct the collar to the desired width and according to the measurements for the neckline and décolleté taken from the finished front and back patterns. Then follow the markings on fig. 2.

Add a seam allowance of 1cm (⅜in.) to the finished pattern, and put in balance and sewing notches.

163

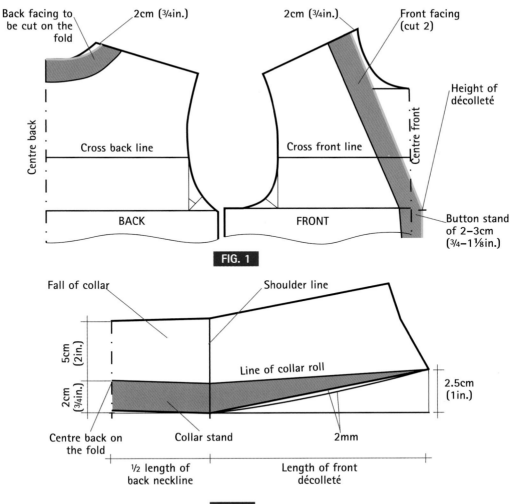

FIG. 1

FIG. 2

Open frilled collar with V-shaped décolleté and front buttoning

Construct the basic bodice pattern according to the measurements given, then make the alterations.

Add a button stand of 3cm (1⅛in.) to the centre front, widen the neckline by 2cm (¾in.) front and back, then mark the depth of the décolleté.

Draw the facings (back and front) with a width of 7–10cm (2¾–4in.) (fig. 1, in violet).

The collar for this style is fitted at the neckline, but frilled along the outside edge. To make this frill easily, use the slashing method. First draw the collar flat on the front pattern (fig. 1, in blue), then trace off the collar shape, which will serve as a basis for the slashing.

164

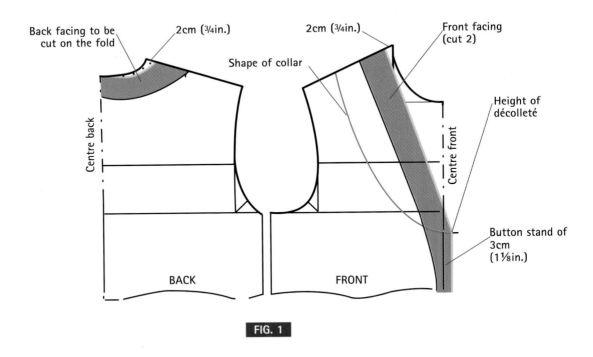

Back facing to be cut on the fold

2cm (¾in.)

Shape of collar

2cm (¾in.)

Front facing (cut 2)

Height of décolleté

Centre back

Centre front

Button stand of 3cm (1⅛in.)

BACK

FRONT

FIG. 1

Place the traced collar pattern (fig. 2, in blue) on another sheet of paper, add the back part (fig. 2, in violet) following the ½ length of the back neckline. Then draw the slash lines (fig. 2).

Spread out the cut pieces at regular intervals (keeping them attached along the inside line of the collar) as shown in fig. 3. Leave the centre back piece vertical along the centre back line.

Then re-draw the collar pattern (fig. 4).

Round off the angles formed by spreading the pieces.

Put in balance and sewing notches and add a seam allowance of 1cm (⅜in.) to the finished pattern.

To prevent the neckline from gaping, apply a stay tape when constructing the garment, as the neckline and the collar are cut on the bias.

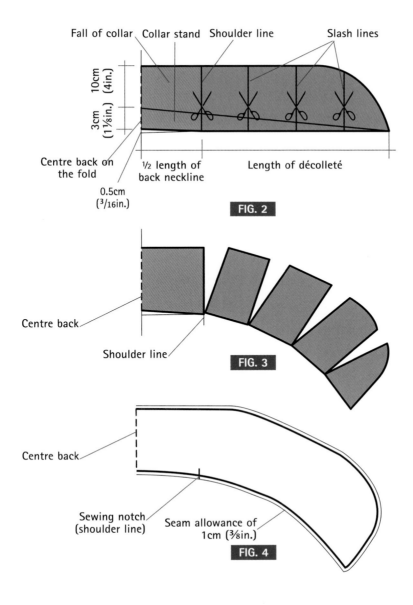

FIG. 2

FIG. 3

FIG. 4

Classic mandarin collar

The mandarin collar is simply the collar stand, enlarged and fitted to the neck. The construction is identical to that of the collar stand for a blouse.

Draw a horizontal line then mark the measurements of the half length of the back neckline and the half length of the front neckline, taken from the finished bodice pattern.

Then follow the markings in fig. 1.

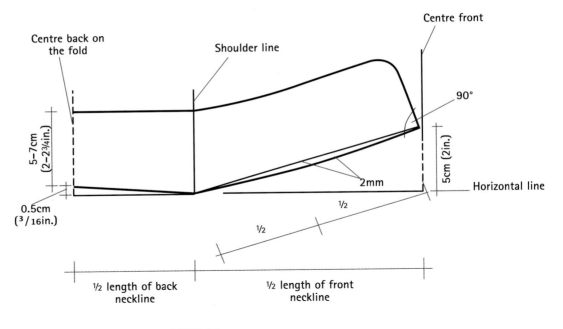

FIG. 1

The mandarin collar can be used equally well on a shirt as on a dress, jacket or coat. The height and fit will depend on its use.

Various slants of the collar line (representing various styles) are shown in figs 2 and 3.

The basic construction of the pattern for the various shapes is identical, the only change being the raising of the point corresponding to the centre front. The colours in fig. 3 correspond to those in fig. 2.

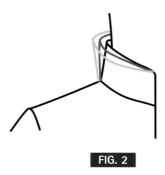

FIG. 2

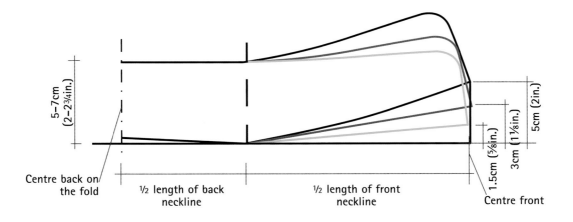

5–7cm (2–2¾in.)

Centre back on the fold

½ length of back neckline

½ length of front neckline

1.5cm (⅝in.)

3cm (1⅛in.)

5cm (2in.)

Centre front

FIG. 3

Shortened mandarin collar

Construct the basic bodice pattern according to the given measurements, then make the alterations.

Add a button stand, with a width no less than 2.5cm (1in.).

Mark the height and shape of the neckline (fig. 1, in green).

Lower the neckline by about 2cm (¾in.) and take it back from the centre front by about 2.5cm (1in.) (fig. 1, in violet).

Draw the new front neckline (fig. 1, in green).

Draw the back and front neck facings about 5–7cm (2–2¾in.) wide (fig. 1, in violet).

Draft the construction lines for the collar, following the markings on fig. 2.

Add a seam allowance of 1cm (⅜in.) to the finished pattern.

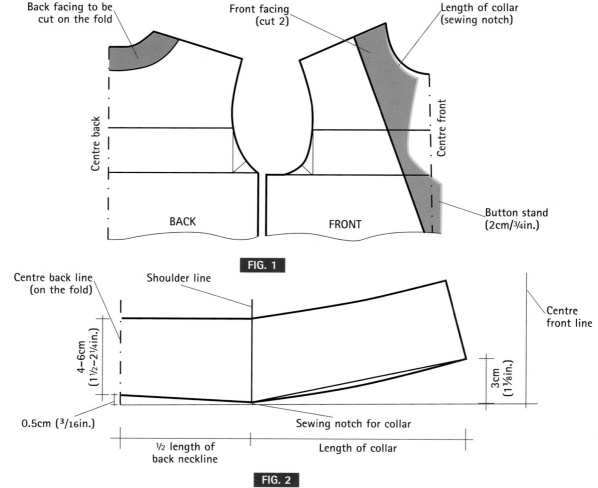

FIG. 1

FIG. 2

Buttoned mandarin collar

Draft first the basic bodice block according to the measurements given.

Draw the shape of the cut out (fig. 1, in green), and then the facings (fig. 1, in violet) to a width of 5–7cm (2–2¾in.).

The construction of the collar is identical to that of the mandarin collar on p.166 (fig. 1), except that a button stand (2.5cm/1in. wide) is added to the centre front.

Add a seam allowance of 1cm (⅜in.) to the finished collar pattern.

Put in the sewing notches.

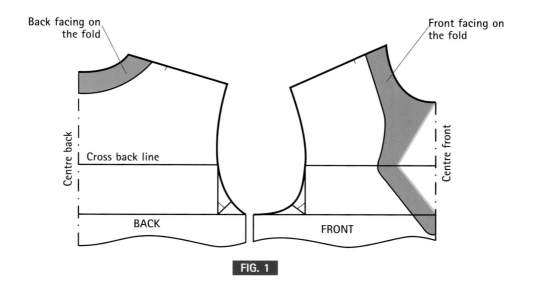

FIG. 1

169

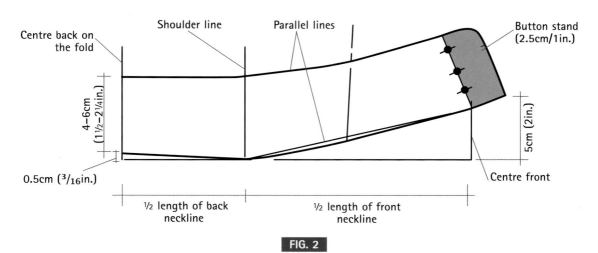

FIG. 2

Peter Pan collar

This is an applied collar around the neckline, drafted directly on to the back and front bodice patterns. All flat collars are constructed in the same way, the only difference is in the design of the fall edges (fig. 1).

To draft a pattern for the chosen collar (see the various shapes suggested in fig. 1) place the basic front and back bodice blocks shoulder to shoulder (fig. 1).

The gap between the two shoulder lines (from 0 at the neckline to 1cm (⅜in.) at the shoulder) prevents the collar pulling and wrinkling after making up the garment.

Then draw the desired shape of collar.

On the centre back and centre front lines lower the collar by 1cm (⅜in.) from the neckline. This will prevent the edge of the collar from riding up after making the garment, producing a slight roll around the neckline (fig. 1).

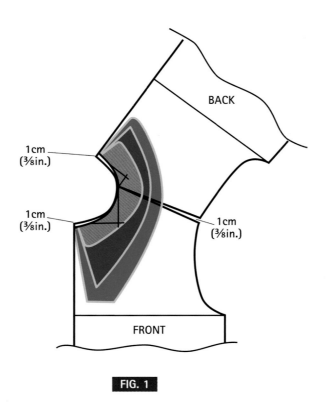

BACK

1cm
(⅜in.)

1cm
(⅜in.)

1cm
(⅜in.)

FRONT

FIG. 1

Flat, asymmetrical collar

Draft the pattern for this collar on the basic bodice block, which has been made according to the given measurements.

As this style is asymmetrical, construct the front left and front right patterns separately. Follow the markings in figs 1 and 2.

Right front
Increase the neckline by 1cm (⅜in.) and extend the point of the neckline according to the shape desired (here, 5cm/2in.). Then draw the button stand which begins at this point and progressively narrows to about 2cm (¾in.) wide at bust level (fig. 1, in violet).

Draw the shape of the collar (in violet) and the facing (the green line). Then trace off the collar and the facing.

Left front
Increase the neckline by 1cm (⅜in.), add a button stand 2cm (¾in.) wide, draw the facing and then trace this out.

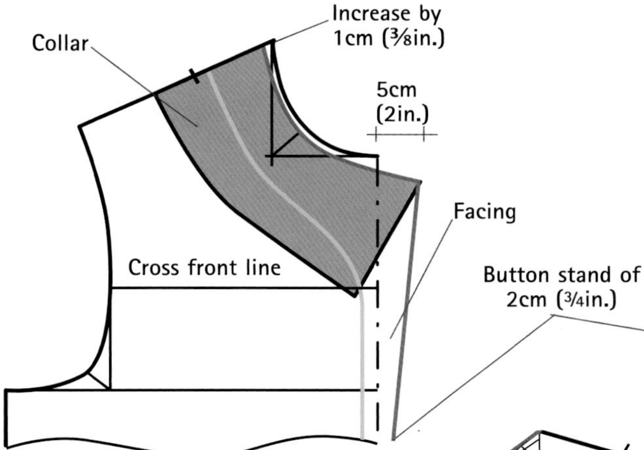

171

Collar · Increase by 1cm (⅜in.) · 5cm (2in.) · Facing · Cross front line · Button stand of 2cm (¾in.)

Front right side.

FIG. 1

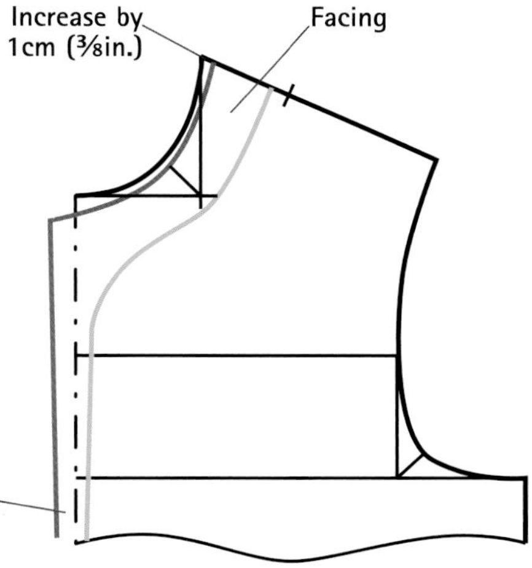

Increase by 1cm (⅜in.) · Facing · Button stand of 2cm (¾in.)

Front left side.

FIG. 2

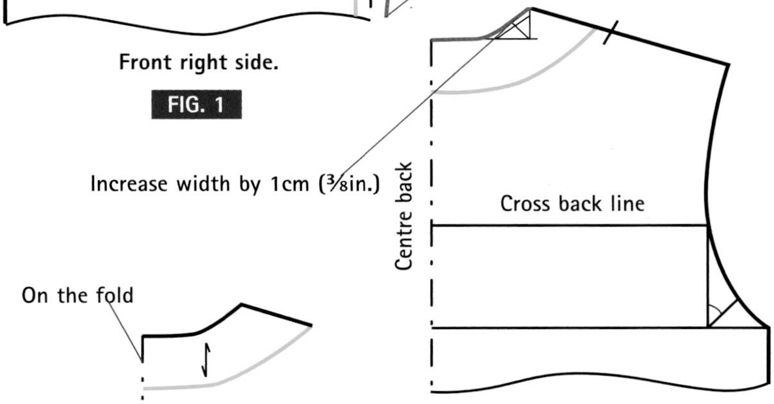

Increase width by 1cm (⅜in.) · Centre back · On the fold

Back pattern.

Cross back line

Back pattern.

FIG. 3

Notches, back, front

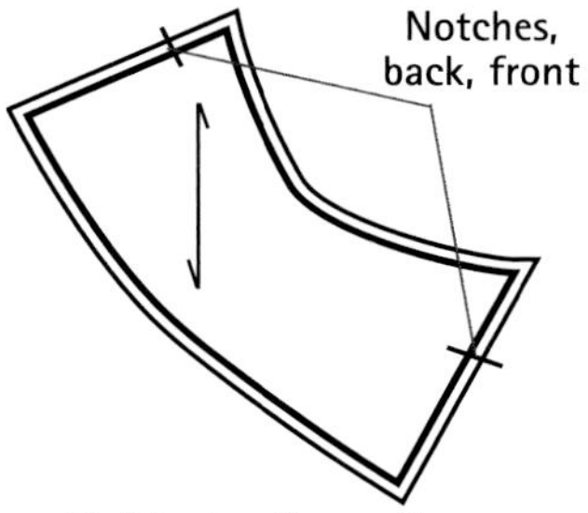

Finished collar pattern.

FIG. 4

Wide, flat collar

Style 11

Construct this pattern on the basic bodice block, drafted according to the given measurements.

Add a button stand of 2cm (¾in.) minimum, then mark the depth of the décolleté.

Place the back and front bodice patterns as shown in fig. 1, then draw the desired shape of collar (fig. 1, in violet).

Draw the facing (fig. 1, in green).

Then trace off the collar and facing.

Put in several balance and sewing notches.

Add a seam allowance of 1cm (⅜in.) to the finished pattern

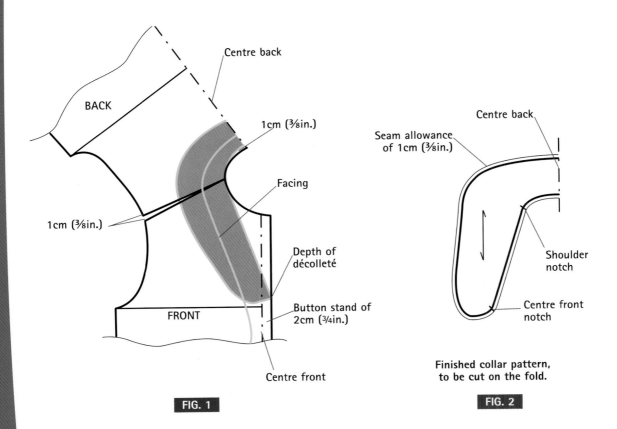

FIG. 1

FIG. 2

Finished collar pattern, to be cut on the fold.

Flat collar with pleats

Construct the pattern for this style in the same way as the collar on p.172.

To obtain a pleat at the edge of the collar, enlarge the base of the collar and widen the shoulder lines by 2cm (¾in.) (fig. 1).

Draw the collar (fig. 1, in green) and the facing (the blue line), then trace them off.

To cut the fall of the collar on the bias, place the centre back of the collar on the straight grain when cutting out.

173

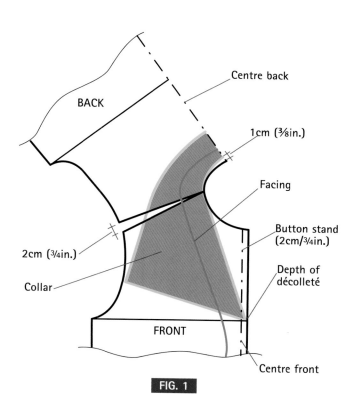

FIG. 1

- Centre back
- BACK
- 1cm (⅜in.)
- Facing
- Button stand (2cm/¾in.)
- Depth of décolleté
- 2cm (¾in.)
- Collar
- FRONT
- Centre front

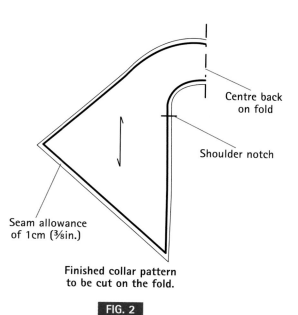

FIG. 2

- Centre back on fold
- Shoulder notch
- Seam allowance of 1cm (⅜in.)
- **Finished collar pattern to be cut on the fold.**

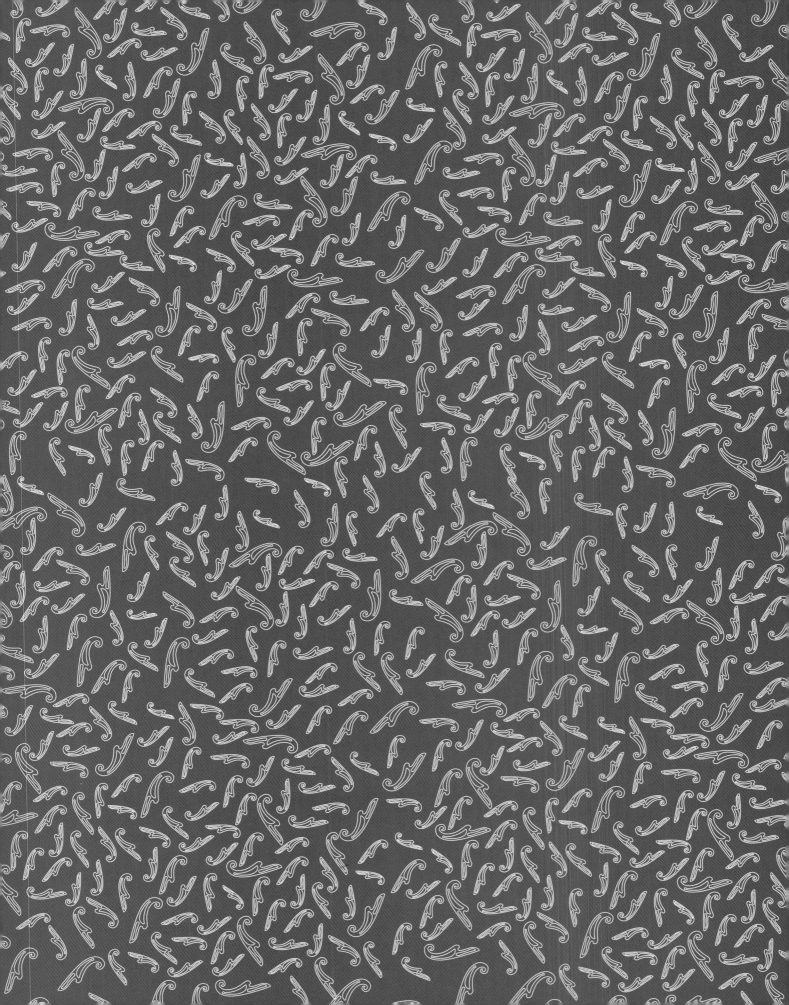

Grown-on collars

This kind of collar is constructed by extending the bodice pattern up to the neck.

Stand-up collars are an extension of the bodice on the neck, without any seams, achieved by some small alterations at the neckline.

Shawl collars are characterised by a V-neck which can be high or low. They are also the only collars where the collar centre back is not on the grain: the slant of this line depends on the width of the collar, which folds back onto the shoulder.

Classic stand-up collar

The stand-up collar is formed by an extension of the back and front up to the neck.

If it is constructed on the basic block neckline, the collar will be close to the neck; for a more comfortable, collar, widen the neckline by 0.5–1cm (³/₁₆–³/₈in.) on the shoulder line.

To give the collar a good shape, adjust the back and front shoulder lines (see alterations in fig. 1).

Design the outside edge of the collar as preferred (see alternative lines shown in colour, fig. 1).

176

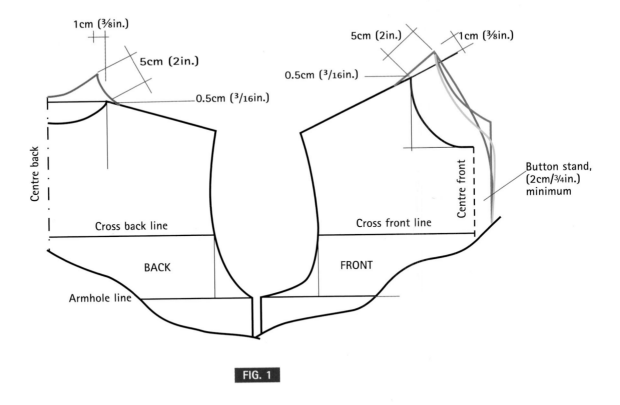

FIG. 1

Stand-up collar with fancy cut-out
Style 2

The curved sections of this collar are not fastened down and risk moving out of shape, so use a fairly firm fabric for the bodice of this style, or interline the facings.

First draft the basic bodice block according to the measurements given, then make the alterations.

Follow the markings in fig. 1.

Add a button stand of 2–3cm (¾–1⅛in.) wide, then draw the desired shape of the cut-out (fig. 1, in green).

Draw the facings to a width of 7–10cm (2¾–4in.) (fig. 1, in violet), and trace them off.

Add a seam allowance of 1cm (⅜in.) to the finished pattern.

Put in several balance and sewing notches.

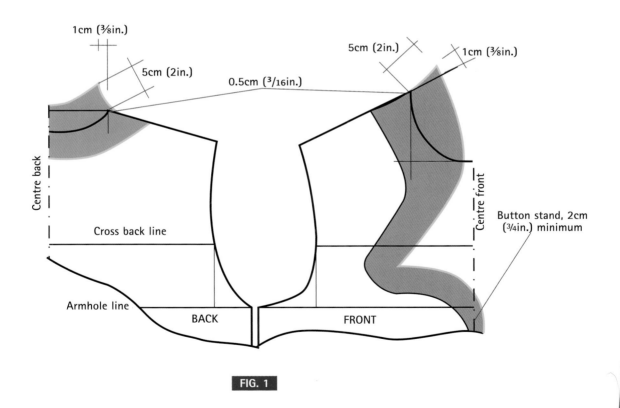

FIG. 1

Asymmetrical stand-up collar

As the front of this style is asymmetrical, construct both left and right of the front pattern.

This style of collar is usually found on garments made from thick fabrics (jackets and coats, for example) so widen the back and front neckline at the shoulder line by 1–2cm (⅜–¾in.). If the style is to be made from a lighter fabric, widen the neckline slightly less (0.5–1cm / ³⁄₁₆–⅜in.).

Back

Draft the basic back bodice block on the fold according to the measurements given. Then construct the collar, following the markings in fig. 1 (in green).

Draw a facing 7–10cm (2¾–4in.) wide (fig. 1, in violet), then trace it off.

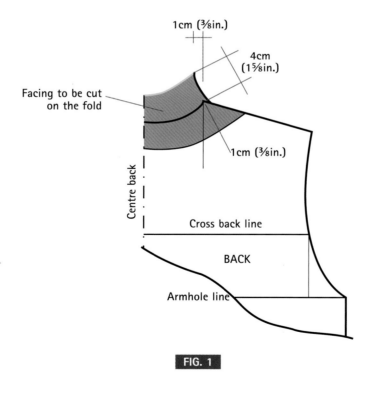

FIG. 1

Front

Draft the basic front bodice block, making the left and right sides separately.

Then make the alterations, shown on fig. 2 (in green).

Draw the facings fairly wide, as the front may be worn open or closed, then trace them off.

Put in several balance and sewing notches.

Add a seam allowance of 1cm (⅜in.) to the finished pattern.

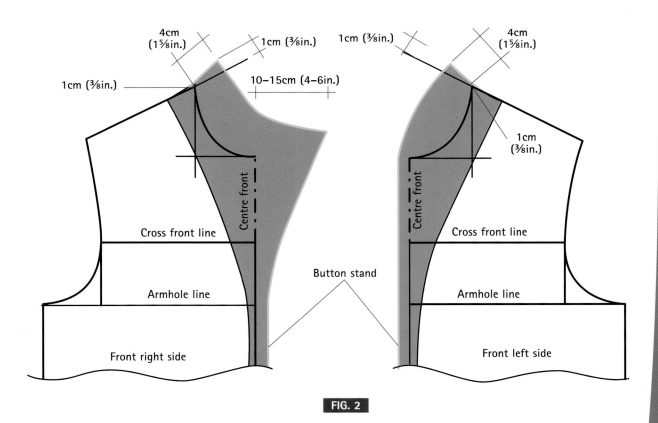

FIG. 2

Stand-up collar with darts

Use a fairly firm fabric, or interline the facing (fig. 1, in violet).

Draft the basic bodice block according to the given measurements, then make the alterations. Mark the depth of the décolleté, then construct the collar (in green) following the markings in fig. 1.

As the stand of the collar is 6cm (2⅜in.), add a dart of 0.5cm (³/₁₆in.) at the front of the neckline to give a better shape.

For a closer-fitting collar, insert a dart near the centre back on the neckline curve (the dart size can be up to 1cm/⅜in. and about 5cm/2in. long).

Put in several balance and sewing notches.

Add a seam allowance of 1cm (⅜in.) to the finished pattern.

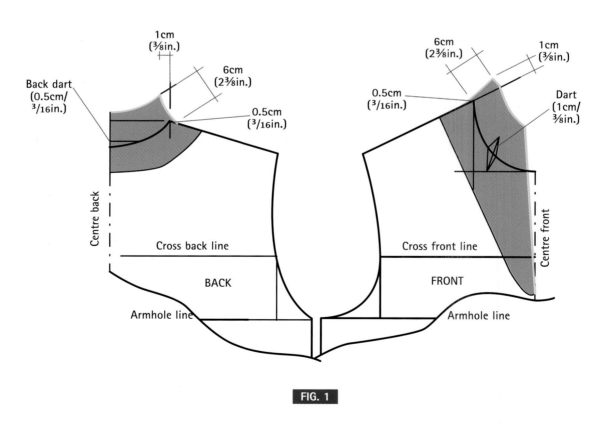

FIG. 1

Stand-up collar with revers

Draft the basic bodice block according to the given measurements, then make the alterations.

On the centre front, add a button stand of 2–3cm (¾–1⅛in.), then draw the lines of construction (in green), following the markings on fig. 1.

Draw the facings (fig. 1, in violet) and trace them off.

Add a seam allowance of 1cm (⅜in.) to the finished pattern.

Put in balance and sewing notches.

181

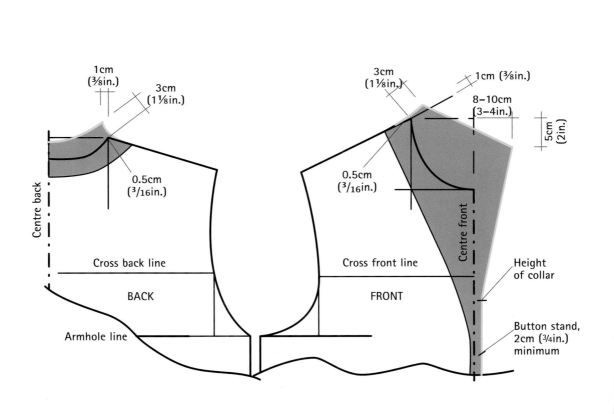

FIG. 1

Stand-up collar with revers on low-cut décolleté

First draft the basic bodice block according to the given measurements, then make the alterations.

Mark the height of the décolleté on the centre front line, as well as its shape.

Construct the collar as shown in fig. 1.

Mark the facings (fig. 1, in violet), then trace them off.

Separate the top and bottom front (fig. 3) along the cutting line.

Add a seam allowance of 1cm (⅜in.) to the finished pattern.

Put in balance and sewing notches.

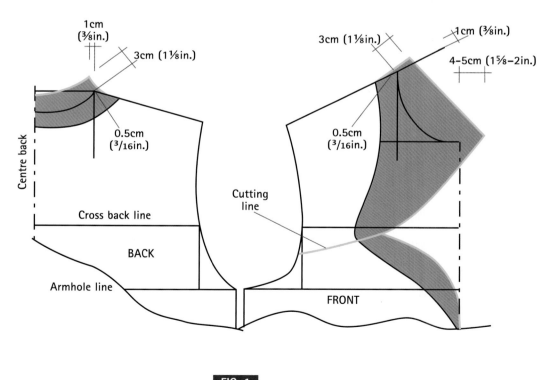

FIG. 1

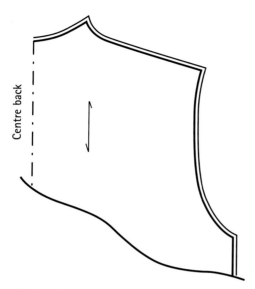

Finished back pattern, to be cut on the fold.

FIG. 2

Finished pattern of back facing,
to be cut on the fold.

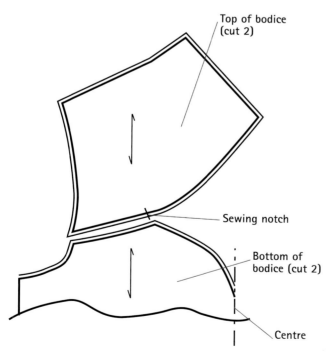

Top of bodice
(cut 2)

Sewing notch

Bottom of
bodice (cut 2)

Centre

Finished front pattern.

FIG. 3

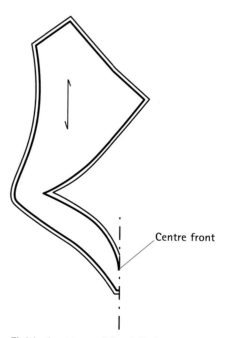

Centre front

Finished pattern of front facing,
to be cut on the fold.

FIG. 4

Classic shawl collar

The back of the classic shawl collar is made by extending the front of the collar.

Construct this pattern on the basic bodice block, drafted to the given measurements, then follow the markings on figs 1 and 2.

Widen the front and back neckline on the shoulder line by 1.5–2cm (⅝–¾in.).

Draw a button stand on the centre front 2–4cm (¾–1⅝in.) wide.

Mark the depth of the décolleté (the break point), then draw a line for the collar roll, starting at the break point and finishing at the enlarged neckline at the shoulder line.

Extend this line by half the length of the back neckline.

Mark a point at 3cm (1⅛in.) parallel to the shoulder line (for the width of the collar stand). Join this point to the shoulder line. Draw a perpendicular line for the centre back 6cm (2⅜in.) (the fall of the collar) beyond the break line.

Draw the outer (leaf) edge of the collar, starting from a right angle at the centre back and joining to the break point.

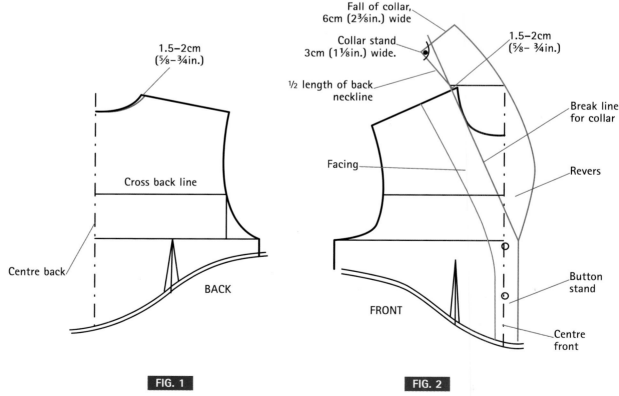

FIG. 1

FIG. 2

184

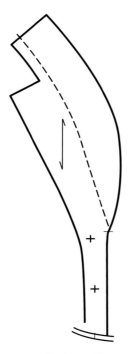

Round off the angles formed during the construction. Trace off the facing. Put in balance and sewing notches. Add a seam allowance of 1cm (⅜in.) to the finished pattern.

**Facing pattern
with collar revers.**

FIG. 3

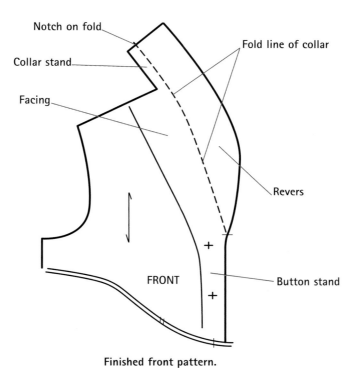

Notch on fold

Collar stand

Facing

Fold line of collar

Revers

FRONT

Button stand

Finished front pattern.

FIG. 4

Pointed shawl collar

Construct the pattern for this style on the adapted bodice block.

The method shown here is different from the method used in the classic shawl collar (pp.184–5).

Draw a button stand 3–4cm (1⅛–1⅝in.) wide, then mark the depth of the décolleté (fig. 2).

Draw the break line for the collar, from the depth of the décolleté (break point) up to the neck at the shoulder line.

Widen the back and front neckline by 2cm (¾in.) on the shoulder line.

On the front pattern draw the shape of the collar (fig. 2, in violet), then, using tracing paper, draw a mirror image of the collar on the other side of the break line (fig. 2, in violet).

Extend the break line by half the length of the back neckline (fig. 3). Mark 3cm (1⅛in.) on a line parallel to the shoulder line. Join this point to the shoulder line, then draw a parallel line at a distance of 2cm (¾in.) (for the collar stand). Finish the back with a perpendicular line of about 6cm (2⅜in.) (the width of the collar fall).

Round off the angles formed during the construction.

186

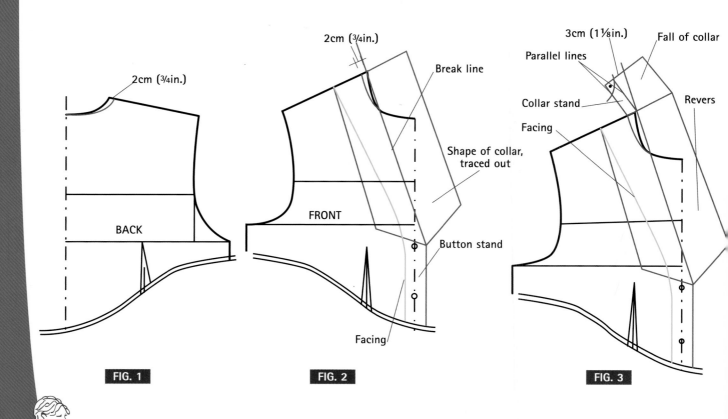

FIG. 1 **FIG. 2** **FIG. 3**

2cm (¾in.)
2cm (¾in.)
Break line
Shape of collar, traced out
FRONT
BACK
Button stand
Facing

3cm (1⅛in.)
Fall of collar
Parallel lines
Collar stand
Facing
Revers

Draft the facing (fig. 4, in green), and trace it off.

Put in balance and sewing notches.

Add a seam allowance of 1cm (⅜in.) to the finished pattern.

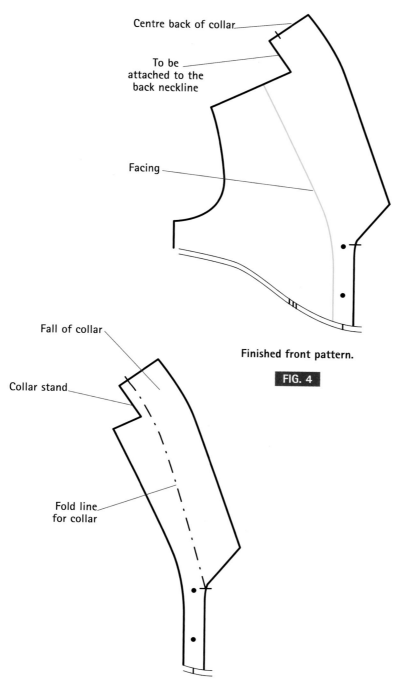

Centre back of collar

To be
attached to the
back neckline

Facing

Finished front pattern.

FIG. 4

Fall of collar

Collar stand

Fold line
for collar

Finished facing pattern.

FIG. 5

187

Short shawl collar

Construct the pattern for this style on the adapted bodice block (fig. 2, in green).

Mark the width of the button stand and the depth of the décolleté.

Widen the neckline front and back by 2cm (¾in.) at the shoulder line. From this point, on the front pattern, extend the top of the shoulder line by 3cm (1⅛in.). From there, draw the break line down to the break point of the décolleté (fig. 2).

Draw the shape of the collar, then use tracing paper to draw a mirror image of the collar on the other side of the break line (fig. 3).

Extend the break line by the half length of the back neckline.

Mark a point at 3cm (1⅜in.) parallel to the shoulder line. Join this point to the shoulder line, then draw a line parallel to this straight line at a distance of 2cm (¾in.) (for the collar stand). Finish the back with a perpendicular line of about 6cm (2¾in.) (the width of collar fall).

Round off the angles formed during the construction.

Draw the facing and trace it off.

Put in balance and sewing notches.

Add a seam allowance of 1cm (⅜in.) to the finished pattern.

188

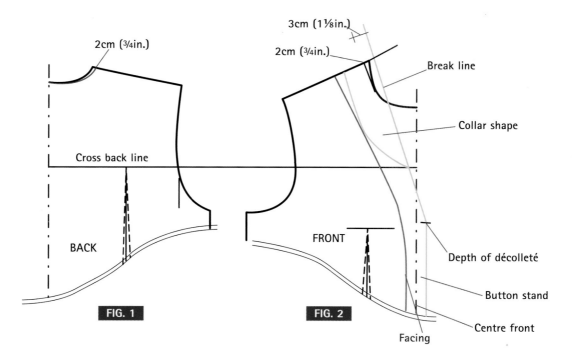

FIG. 1
FIG. 2

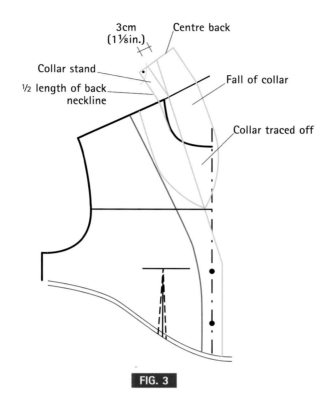

3cm
(1⅛in.)

Centre back

Collar stand

Fall of collar

½ length of back
neckline

Collar traced off

FIG. 3

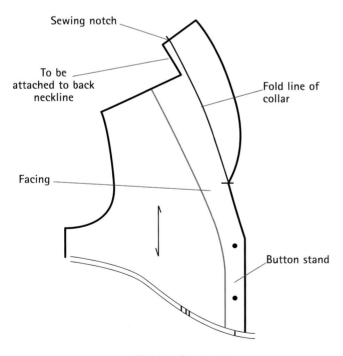

Sewing notch

To be
attached to back
neckline

Fold line of
collar

Facing

Button stand

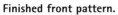

Finished front pattern.

FIG. 4

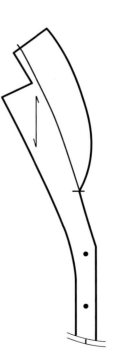

Finished facing pattern.

FIG. 5

COLLARS

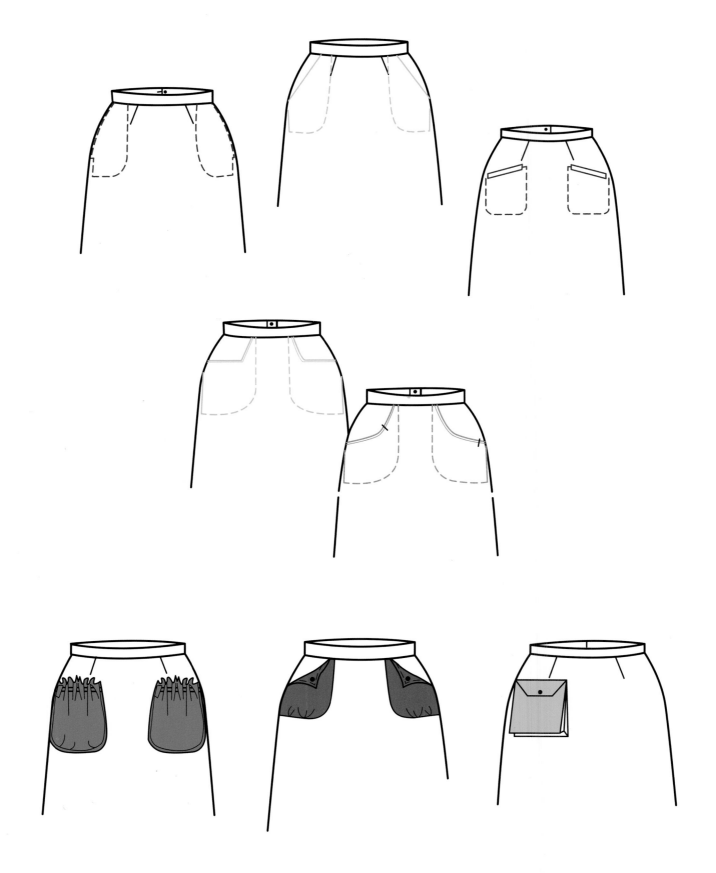

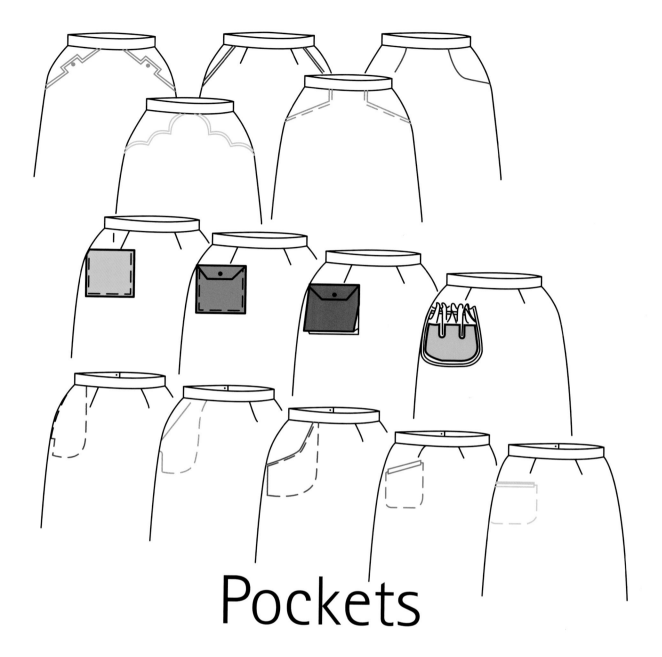

Pockets

Pocket styles can be divided into two distinct categories: structural pockets (p.195) and applied pockets (p.207).

Whatever its style or shape, a pocket must be placed somewhere comfortable and accessible, unless it only has a decorative function.

A basic pattern or method of construction on which to base the pocket pattern does not really exist. There follow some indications and advice about particular styles of pockets, but there is no reason not to use alternative methods to those described in this chapter.

Method for cutting out
a structural pocket

First, mark the length of the opening: the hand must be able to slip inside without any difficulty. For example, if the finished opening of the pocket is 15cm, draw a line 13cm long (the other 2cm being for the seam allowance added at each side).

Fold the cut pieces back on the fold line to reveal the pocket opening (fig. 2).

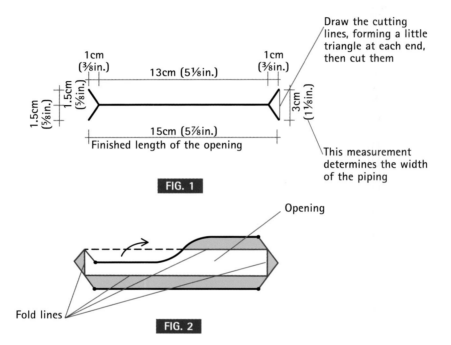

FIG. 1

FIG. 2

Before cutting the opening, check the final size required.

Apply the piping: if it is single, it will cover the whole opening (fig. 3), but if it is double, each length of piping (top and bottom) will cover half the opening (fig. 4).

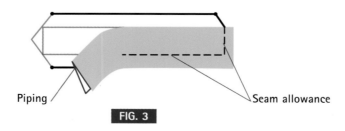

FIG. 3

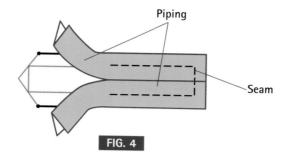

FIG. 4

Finishes

The opening of a pocket made in a seam is generally finished with a piping called jetting, or a welt to cover the two seam edges.

The finish is determined by the type of garment and the choice of fabric.

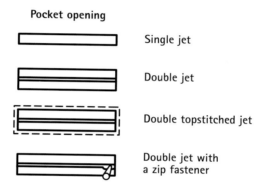

Pocket opening

Single jet

Double jet

Double topstitched jet

Double jet with
a zip fastener

Shape of edges for slanting pockets

The edge can be designed to any shape, whatever the style of slanting pocket used or type of garment on which the pocket is made.

Different edge designs for structural pockets.

FIG. 1

Whether the pockets are placed in a bodice, skirt, jacket, dress or coat the construction methods stay the same.

Structural pockets

Structural pockets are inserted into a seam, or inset, and are hidden inside the garment. The only visible part of this kind of pocket is the opening, so there is no scope for using structural pockets to personalise a garment or express your creativity.

The construction of a structural pocket is more complex than that of an applied pocket, and varies according to its placement.

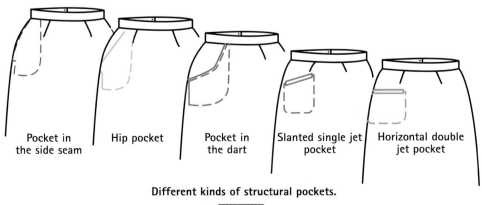

Pocket in the side seam | Hip pocket | Pocket in the dart | Slanted single jet pocket | Horizontal double jet pocket

Different kinds of structural pockets.

FIG. 1

Pocket bag

Opening

Pocket in the side seam of a skirt

This pocket is sewn in the skirt side seam.

Draw the shape of the pocket on the finished skirt pattern (fig. 1, in green).

Put in notches to mark the position and width of the opening (here about 12cm/4¾in.).

Then trace off the shape of the pocket bag (fig. 2) and draw a facing (in blue). This facing is cut from the fabric so that the lining of the pocket doesn't show when open.

Then separate the facing and bottom of the pocket pieces (fig. 3). The pocket bag is cut from lining fabric to avoid too much thickness of fabric.

Add a seam allowance of 1cm (⅜in.) to the finished pattern.

196

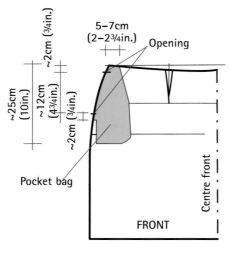

Skirt pattern:
pocket position.

FIG. 1

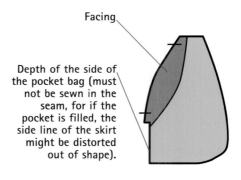

Facing

Depth of the side of the pocket bag (must not be sewn in the seam, for if the pocket is filled, the side line of the skirt might be distorted out of shape).

Shape of the pocket.

FIG. 2

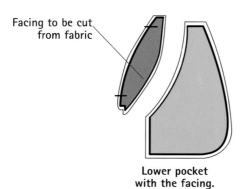

Facing to be cut from fabric

Lower pocket with the facing.

FIG. 3

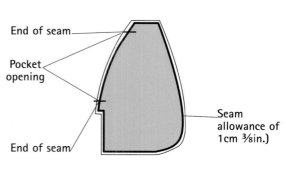

End of seam

Pocket opening

Seam allowance of 1cm ⅜in.)

End of seam

Top of the pocket bag.

FIG. 4

PATTERN-DRAFTING FOR FASHION: THE BASICS

Inset skirt pocket

In general the opening of this style is finished with piping or a welt to cover the two pocket seams (which are positioned about 2cm/¾in. apart).

Draw the opening for the pocket (see pp.192–3) and the shape of the pocket bag on the finished skirt pattern (fig. 1).

Trace off the shape of the pocket bag.

Add a seam allowance of 1cm (⅜in.) to each part.

Put in balance and sewing notches.

Pocket bag

Welt of 2cm (¾in.)

197

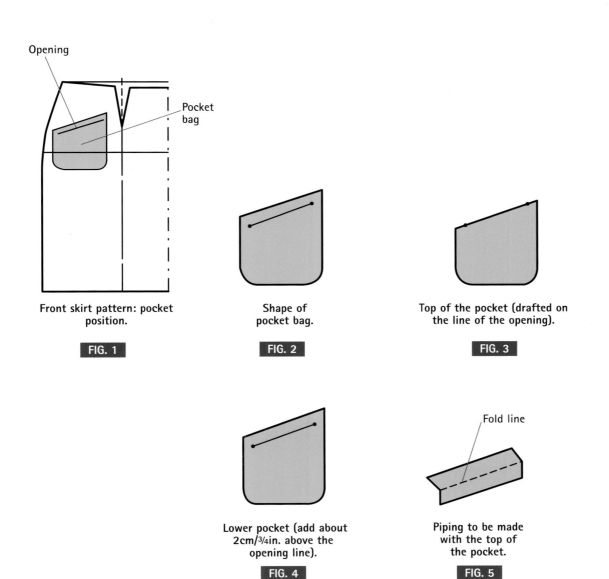

Front skirt pattern: pocket position.

FIG. 1

Shape of pocket bag.

FIG. 2

Top of the pocket (drafted on the line of the opening).

FIG. 3

Lower pocket (add about 2cm/¾in. above the opening line).

FIG. 4

Piping to be made with the top of the pocket.

FIG. 5

Pocket in the front dart of a skirt

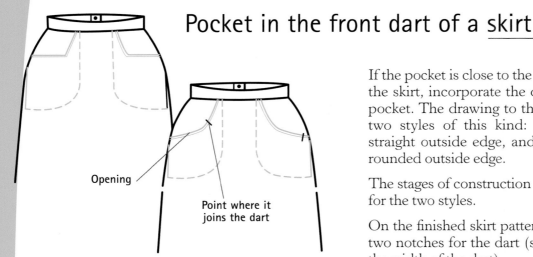

Opening

Point where it
joins the dart

If the pocket is close to the front dart of
the skirt, incorporate the dart into the
pocket. The drawing to the left shows
two styles of this kind: one with a
straight outside edge, and one with a
rounded outside edge.

The stages of construction are identical
for the two styles.

On the finished skirt pattern put in the
two notches for the dart (separated by
the width of the dart).

Draw the pocket opening, starting from
the first notch (fig. 1, in orange) and
draw the dart from the second notch,
joining the pocket opening (orange line
on fig. 1).

Then trace off the shape of the pocket
with the side of the skirt (fig. 2).

To keep the width of the dart, which will
be included in the pocket, move the dart
as shown in fig 3. Then remove the dart.

198

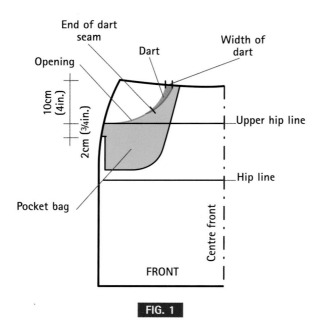

End of dart
seam

Width of
dart

Dart

Opening

10cm (4in.)

2cm (¾in.)

Upper hip line

Pocket bag

Hip line

Centre front

FRONT

FIG. 1

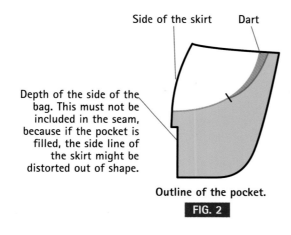

Side of the skirt   Dart

Depth of the side of the
bag. This must not be
included in the seam,
because if the pocket is
filled, the side line of
the skirt might be
distorted out of shape.

Outline of the pocket.

FIG. 2

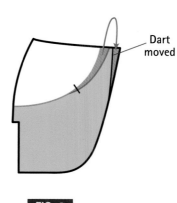

Dart
moved

FIG. 3

On the new outline of the pocket draw the line of the facing (fig. 4). This facing is grown on to the hip section of the skirt and is cut in fabric so that the lining does not show when the pocket is open (fig. 6).

Separate the two pieces of the lower pocket (the hip section with the facing and the bottom of the pocket) and then add a seam allowance of 1cm (⅜in.) around all the pieces of the pocket (figs 6 and 7).

Put in balance and sewing notches.

To avoid unnecessary thickness of fabric, cut out the top and lower pocket bag in lining fabric.

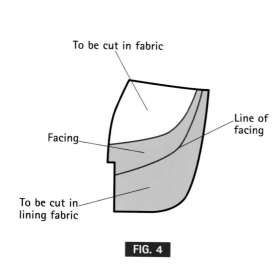

FIG. 4

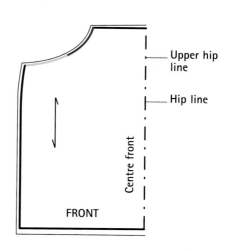

Finished front skirt pattern.

FIG. 5

199

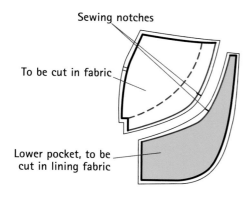

Hip section with the grown-on facing and the lower pocket.

FIG. 6

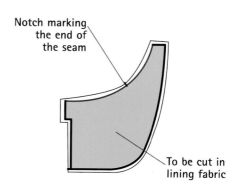

Top pocket.

FIG. 7

Edge of pocket
(opening)

Pocket bag

Hip pocket

Draw the edge of the pocket in the desired place on the basic pattern (fig. 1).

Then trace off the pocket bag (fig. 2).

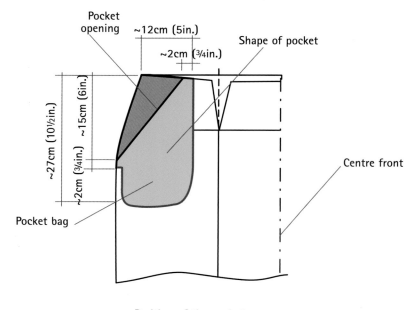

Position of the pocket on
the basic pattern.

FIG. 1

Draw a line parallel to the line of the opening, at a distance of 2–5cm (¾–2in.) for the facing (fig. 2).

Then, trace off the separate pieces: the hip section with the grown-on facing, and the top and lower pocket (figs 3 and 4).

Cut the top and lower pocket in lining fabric to avoid unnecessary thickness of fabric (figs 3 and 4). Cut the facing in fabric so that the lining does not show when the pocket is opened. The lower pocket can be cut in fabric: if doing so, include the facing (which is no longer necessary) in the lower pocket pattern.

Add a seam allowance of 1cm (⅜in.).

Put in balance and sewing notches on the finished pocket pattern.

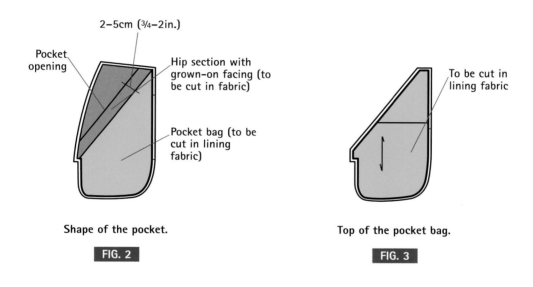

Shape of the pocket.

FIG. 2

Top of the pocket bag.

FIG. 3

201

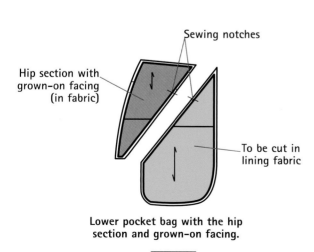

Lower pocket bag with the hip section and grown-on facing.

FIG. 4

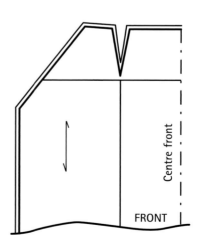

Finished skirt pattern.

FIG. 5

Pocket in the vertical seam of a jacket

On the finished bodice pattern mark the pocket opening (which should be sufficiently wide for the hand) as shown in fig. 1, then draw the shape of the pocket bag (fig. 1, in green).

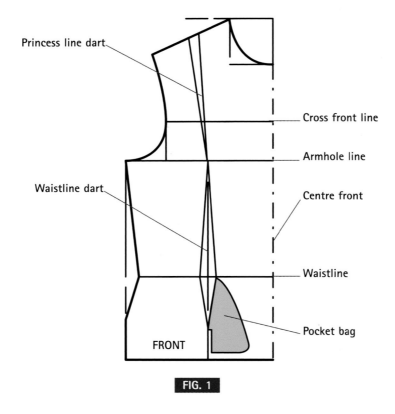

Princess line dart

Waistline dart

Cross front line

Armhole line

Centre front

Waistline

Pocket bag

FRONT

FIG. 1

Trace off the shape of the pocket (fig. 2).

Draw the facing (2–3cm/¾–1⅛in. wide). It will be cut in fabric so that the lining is not visible when the pocket is opened (fig. 2, in blue).

Then trace off all the separate pieces: facing, top and lower pocket (figs 3 and 4).

The pocket bag must be cut in lining fabric to avoid excess thickness of fabric (figs 3 and 4, in green).

Add a seam allowance of 1cm (⅜in.) to each piece.

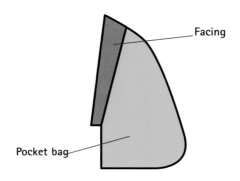

Facing

Pocket bag

Shape of the pocket.

FIG. 2

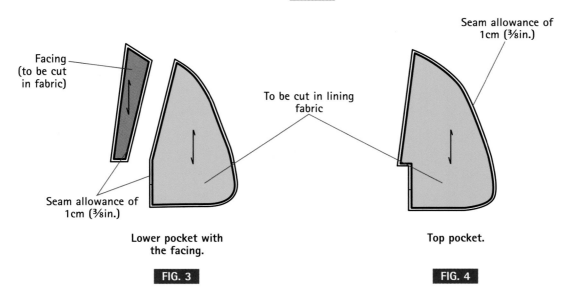

Facing
(to be cut
in fabric)

To be cut in lining
fabric

Seam allowance of
1cm (⅜in.)

Seam allowance of
1cm (⅜in.)

**Lower pocket with
the facing.**

Top pocket.

FIG. 3

FIG. 4

POCKETS

Pocket in the horizontal seam of a jacket

To construct this style of pocket, first draft the finished bodice pattern, then make the alterations. Draw the opening line of the pocket and the outline of the pocket as shown in fig. 1.

Trace off all of the pieces (figs 2 and 3).

As the pocket does not have piping, extend the side front by a sufficient width of facing so that the seam of the lower pocket is not visible (fig. 2, in blue). The facing has already been attached to the pocket outline (fig. 3).

204

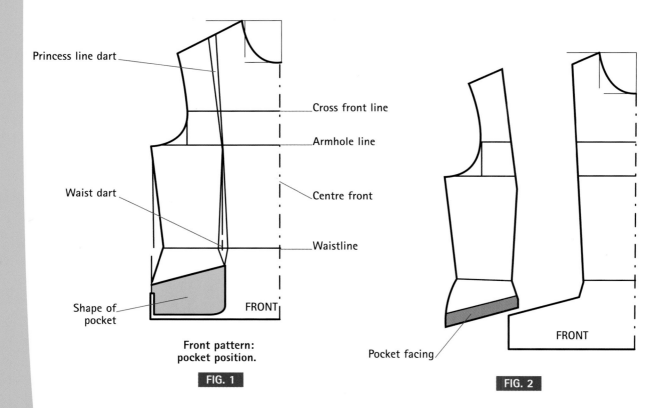

FIG. 1

Princess line dart

Cross front line

Armhole line

Centre front

Waistline

Waist dart

Shape of pocket

FRONT

Front pattern: pocket position.

FIG. 2

Pocket facing

FRONT

Cut the pocket bag in lining fabric to avoid excess thickness of fabric.

Add a seam allowance of 1cm (⅜in.) to each piece.

Put in balance and sewing notches.

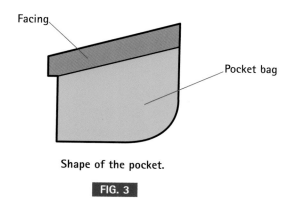

Facing

Pocket bag

Shape of the pocket.

FIG. 3

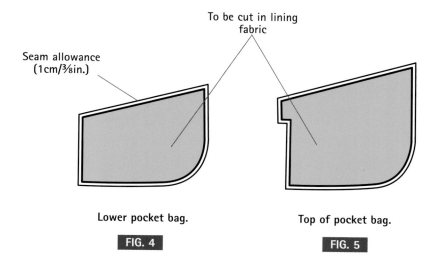

To be cut in lining fabric

Seam allowance
(1cm/⅜in.)

Lower pocket bag.

FIG. 4

Top of pocket bag.

FIG. 5

Applied (or patch) pockets

Applied pockets are simply sewn onto the garment, and only need careful marking for their placement. They can be constructed entirely 'on the flat' but it is a good idea to cut them out in a fabric such as calico to be certain of the size and positioning.

This style of pocket has great scope for creativity because of the large number of possible shapes, and so enables the garment to be personalised. The pockets can be both decorative and useful, and ease of use should be carefully considered.

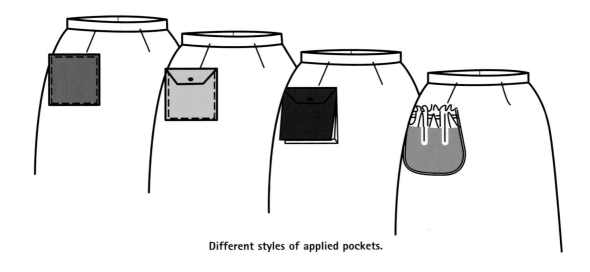

Different styles of applied pockets.

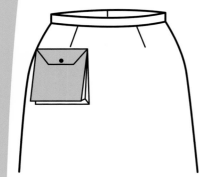

Pocket with a gusset and flap

Mark the dimensions of the pocket so it has a comfortable opening for the hand (14–16cm/5½–6¼in. wide). Then add the required gusset depth at the sides and bottom of the pocket (here, about 4cm/1⅝in., fig. 2).

To avoid excess thickness of fabric at the corners of the pocket, trim off the surplus by cutting across the angles (see fig. 2).

Add a seam allowance of 1cm (⅜in.) at the sides and bottom, as well as a hem of 2cm (¾in.) at the opening.

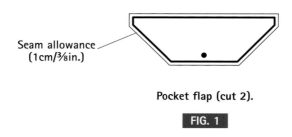

Seam allowance (1cm/⅜in.)

Pocket flap (cut 2).

FIG. 1

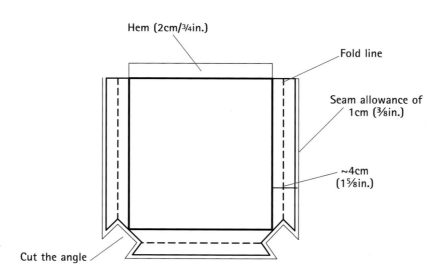

Hem (2cm/¾in.)

Fold line

Seam allowance of 1cm (⅜in.)

~4cm (1⅝in.)

Cut the angle

Finished pattern of the pocket.

FIG. 2

208

Puff pocket with revers

Style 2

Mark the dimensions of the pocket with a comfortable opening for the hand (for example, 14–16cm/5½–6¼in. wide).

To achieve a puffed effect at the bottom of the pocket, put in a few pleats, each 1–2cm (⅜–¾in.) wide. Then construct a facing for the revers (fig. 1).

Trace off the revers from the fold line, then add 2–3cm (¾–1⅛in.) (fig. 2). This part will be sewn into the waist and side seams.

Put in balance and sewing notches and add a seam allowance and a hem.

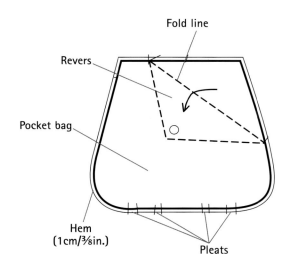

Finished pattern of the pocket.

FIG. 1

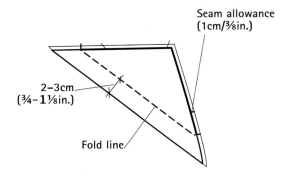

Facing for revers.

FIG. 2

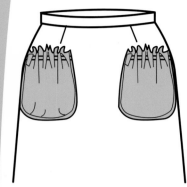

Fancy pocket with gathered opening

Mark the dimensions of the pocket with a comfortable opening for the hand (for example, 14–16cm/5½–6¼in. wide). Increase this opening at each side by half the width of the pocket (that is, double the width), which will create the gathers when the opening is pulled in.

Trace off the top part of the pocket to make a facing.

Mark the position of the buttonholes to insert the gathering ribbon.

Add a seam allowance and a hem.

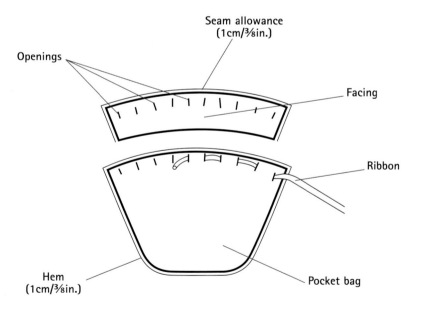

Openings

Seam allowance
(1cm/⅜in.)

Facing

Ribbon

Pocket bag

Hem
(1cm/⅜in.)

Finished pocket pattern.

FIG. 1

The lining

The lining of a garment is more or less a perfect copy, with a few alterations. All garments can be lined fully or partially, whether for practical, aesthetic or technical reasons.

Practical reasons to line a garment :
— to make it comfortable to wear
— to reinforce a garment made in very delicate fabric

Aesthetic reasons to line a garment :
— a decorative linings may be used to embellish a garment (for example, some companies use linings stamped with their logo)
— to conceal the transparency of certain styles or to play with colour contrasts through transparent fabrics

Technical reasons to line a garment :
— to make the garment warmer, the lining being made in thick fabric like wool or fur
— to conceal the different interior structures of a style, such as stays or shoulder pads
— to conceal the inside seams

Whatever kind of garment it is, the lining must always be comfortable and allow ease of movement.

Skirt linings

Inserting the lining

During assembly, the skirt and its lining are inserted at the same time into the waistband. The lining darts can be sewn up or simply folded, but must always be positioned at exactly the same place as the darts of the skirt. This avoids problems during wear and ensures the same hang for the skirt and its lining. When the skirt is made of thick fabric, it is better to alternate the direction of the skirt darts and the lining darts.

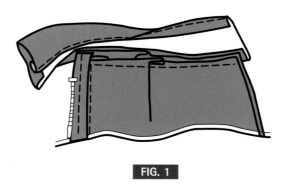

FIG. 1

Classic skirt lining

The lining for a straight skirt or flared skirt is made on the same pattern as that of the skirt – only the length is different. In ready-to-wear skirts, the linings are loose, that is, they are only secured at the waistband.

In haute couture, the lining is often 'bagged out', or fastened by a seam at the hem.

FIG. 2

FIG. 3

Lining for full skirts

The lining for full skirts (circular, pleated, etc.) is not made on the same pattern as the skirts, for the sake of comfort. They are made on the pattern for a flared skirt, with slits at the sides if necessary for ease of movement.

FIG. 4

Lining for long skirts

In the case of a long skirt, it is better not to make the lining the same length, in order to keep the skirt fluid at the bottom. The lining is made on the straight skirt pattern, to knee length, and provided with slits at the sides if necessary.

Lining for a jacket or coat

To make sure the lining fits well and is comfortable, it is necessary to make some modifications to the finished bodice pattern before drafting the lining pattern.

1. Omit the facing from the finished pattern (fig. 1, in violet). The facing will be cut afterwards in the fabric of the garment.

2. Enlarge the pattern by 2 – 3cm (¾–1⅛cm) at the centre back line, in order to obtain what is known as the ease pleat. This will be secured at the top by the facing and at the bottom by the hem, in the form of a flat or inverted pleat (fig. 3).

3. If the garment has shoulder pads, lift the lining pattern by the thickness of the pads (fig. 1, in green).

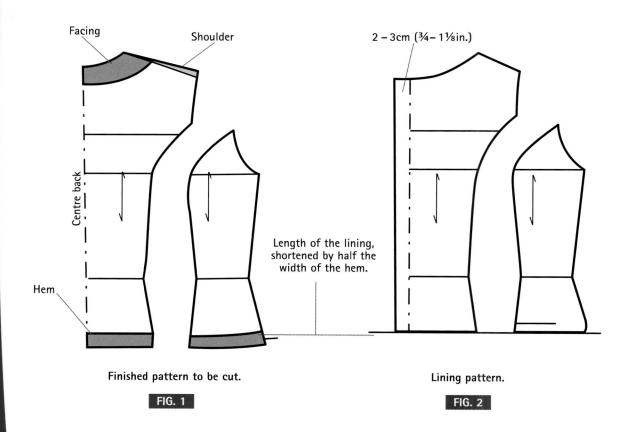

Finished pattern to be cut.

FIG. 1

Lining pattern.

FIG. 2

Shorten the length of the lining by half the width of the hem. For example, hem length = 5cm; 5 ÷ 2 = 2.5cm. The lining will now be shorter than the garment by 2.5cm (figs 1 and 2).

For a lined garment make a hem of at least 3cm (1⅛in.), so that the lining will not show below the garment once the extra ease has been added at the hem (fig. 4).

Add a 1cm (⅜in.) seam allowance.

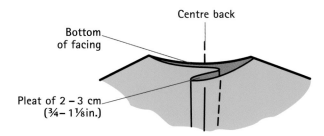

Lining pleat at centre back.

FIG. 3

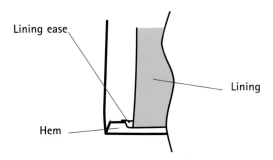

Lining ease at the foot of the garment.

FIG. 4

Cross-section of seams

Finished patterns must have useful instructions on the next stage of making up the garment. They should include cross-section diagrams of the seams required in assembly. These are the most commonly used basic seam diagrams.

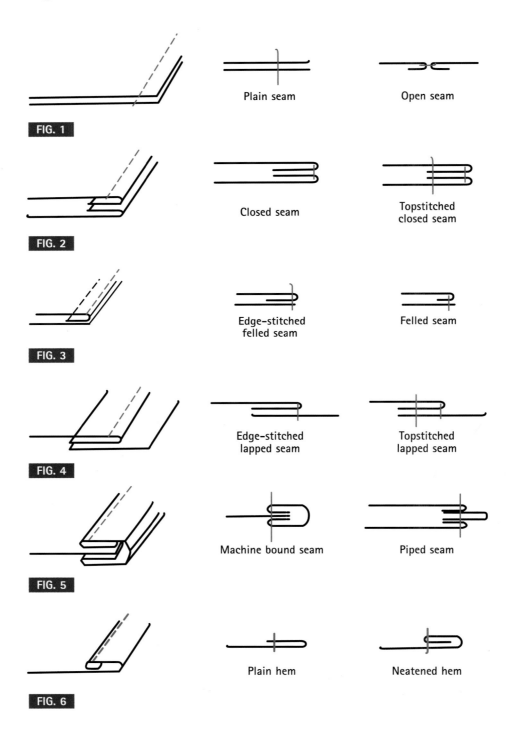

FIG. 1

Plain seam

Open seam

FIG. 2

Closed seam

Topstitched closed seam

FIG. 3

Edge-stitched felled seam

Felled seam

FIG. 4

Edge-stitched lapped seam

Topstitched lapped seam

FIG. 5

Machine bound seam

Piped seam

FIG. 6

Plain hem

Neatened hem

Glossary

Adjust To adapt a garment to the measurements required.

Appliqué A piece of fabric or accessory attached to another fabric.

Armscye The armhole opening in a garment.

Bag out Place two pieces of fabric, right sides together. Sew all around, leaving an opening, then turn right side out.

Balance The correct hang of a garment cut with the warp (vertical) grain of the fabric, and the weft (horizontal) grain.

Balance notch Small nick at the edge of a pattern piece which helps to position it correctly.

Basque Short extension to a bodice or jacket from the waist down to the hips.

Bias Diagonal, 45° line between the warp (vertical) and weft (horizontal) grains of the fabric. Bias tape or binding is made at this 45° angle. False bias is a line drawn which is not at 45°.

Boning stay Flexible rod of metal or plastic used to reinforce and support a garment (see Vol 2 , Fitted bodices, p.219.).

Break line The line along which the lapel rolls back. *See also* Fold

Break point Point on the neckline where the revers turns back to form the lapel.

Button Small piece of metal, wood etc used to fasten garments.

Buttonhole Slit made manually or by machine in a garment to allow a button through.

Button stand Small piece added to an edge on which the buttons and buttonholes are to be placed.

Collar Piece of fabric added to a garment at the neckline, and which surrounds the neck or décolleté (see Vol 1, Collars, p.149).

Collar stand Part of the collar from neckline to roll line (see Vol 1, Collars, p.149).

Crotch Line which divides the left and right parts of the pelvis, going from the centre back waist, through the fork between the legs to the centre front (see Vol 2, Trousers, p.149).

Curve To draw a curved line.

Cut off grain To rebalance part of a garment by changing the grain of the fabric.

Dart Pleat sewn inside to adjust a garment (see Vol 1, Darts, p.21).

Décolleté Low-cut neckline, either for convenience or decorative effect (see Vol 1, Low necklines, p.33).

Drape To arrange fabric gracefully in soft, irregular pleats and folds.

Ease Extra measure added to the rounded length at the head of the sleeve, necessary for the natural roundness of the arm (see Vol 1, Ease, p.29). *See also* Tolerance

Facing Piece of fabric lining a neckline, armhole etc., to finish it off. When used on a lapel, it allows this to be folded over to the right side.

Fall of a collar Depth of the collar from the roll line down to the garment.

Fitted form Term used for a piece added inside a garment that has the shape of the original, such as a waistband or a facing (see Vol 1, Skirts, p.118).

Flare To open out or enlarge part of a garment (for example the bottom of a skirt).

Flat pattern cutting Technique of making a pattern for a garment by making a draft and constructing the pattern pieces on paper.

Flounce An added band of fabric in the shape of a circle or spiral, which can be frilled, folded, or on the bias (see Vol 1, Skirt with flounces, p.142).

219

Fold line or break line Line on which a piece of fabric is folded back (for example, the revers of a collar).

Fork The point of a pair of trousers at which the legs join.

French curve Curved ruler used to draw curves.

Fullness Volume given to a garment, in whole or in part.

Gather To sew along a piece of fabric with a loose stitch and then pull the thread to reduce the width of part of a garment.

Godet False pleat formed by a bias cut, or very often by the addition of a piece of fabric in the shape of a triangle – added to a skirt for extra fullness at the hem (see Vol 1, Skirt with godets, p.138).

Grading Faithful reproduction of a basic pattern block in smaller or larger sizes (see Vol 2, Grading, p.14).

Grain Direction of the threads in a woven fabric. The warp is the vertical threads down the length of a piece of fabric. The weft is the horizontal threads woven in between the vertical warp.

Grown-on Term indicating that the part in question is an integral part of the garment, as opposed to 'separate' (for example, the shawl collar is cut 'grown-on', or as one pattern piece with the garment).

Gusset Piece of fabric placed under the arms to give ease to a kimono sleeve (see Vol 2, Kimonos, p.73).

Hang The drape and flow of a garment – the result of a good cut and careful making up.

Hem Finish at the edge of a garment which involves turning up (or in) some fabric to the inside.

Hollow out To increase the depth of a dart or seam. Used to enlarge a neckline or armhole.

Inside leg Inside leg measurement taken from the crotch down to the ground (see Vol 2, Trousers, p.149).

Lining Copy of a garment cut in fabric which is generally much finer. Inserted inside a garment to hide the inside seams, to give it more body, and sometimes to add warmth (see Vol 1, The lining, p.213).

Loop Little ring of plaited thread or fabric attached to the edge of a garment, to be used with buttons.

Making up To assemble the different pieces of a garment (for example, to fit the sleeve around the armhole).

Mitre Diagonal cut made in a corner where two pieces of fabric are joined, in order to avoid too much thickness of fabric.

Modelling In fashion, concept and construction of a garment, working from a design sketch to create a pattern and then using either flat cutting or draping on the stand.

Neckline Opening at the top of the bodice to let the head through; curved line around the neck.

Notch To make small cuts along a seam to give it flexibility (for example, on a curve or angle).

On the fold Term written on the centre of a half pattern where there is no seam. The centre of the pattern piece is placed on the fold of the fabric, on the grain.

Pattern Model in paper, card or fabric used as a base for cutting out a garment.

Piping Length of fabric cut on the bias which is turned over an edge. Used to decorate buttonholes and pockets (see Vol 1, Pockets, p.191).

Placket Separate piece of fabric used to hide a slit or opening.

Pleat Piece of fabric folded back on itself.

Press-stud Fastening device in metal or plastic, one part has a small knob that snaps into a hole on the other part.

Revers Band of fabric folded back onto the right side of the garment. For example, at the bottom of trousers (also called a turn-up), bottom of a sleeve, or part of the front neckline folded back with the

220

facing to make a collar revers.

Rise (trousers) Exterior length of the leg from the waist to the crotch between the legs (see Vol 2, Trousers, p.149).

Selvege Edge of the fabric, formed by the return of the weft threads.

Sewing notch Small nick at the edge of a garment piece which can then be matched with others when making up. This helps to keep the balance and hang of the garment.

Shoulder pad Little semi-circular cushion placed on the shoulder at the edge of the armhole to give volume and add height to the shoulder.

Slashing technique Means of introducing extra volume (for example, in a sleeve) by dividing the area into vertical or 'sunray' sections, slashing (cutting) almost to the top and then spreading out the cut sections to the desired fullness.

Style line Line or seam drawn for a decorative or functional effect.

To take in (at the waist) To suppress the volume of fabric at the waist by means of seams or darts (see Vol 2, Jacket styles, p47).

Tolerance Width, flexibility and volume added to the basic garment to make it more comfortable (see Vol 1, Tolerance, p.27).

Turn-up/Turn-back Piece of a lined garment that can be folded back.

Warp see Grain

Weft see Grain

Wrist Foot of a long sleeve ending with a turn-back, hem or cuff.

Yoke Piece added to a garment, marked by a seam, for a decorative effect or a particular style.

221

Expanded contents

222

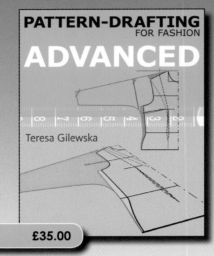
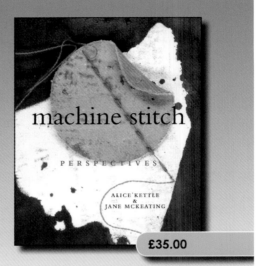
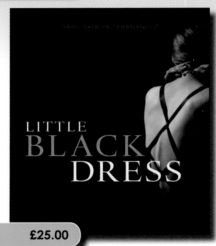